Development as Communication

A PERSPECTIVE ON INDIA

Uma Narula and W. Barnett Pearce

Southern Illinois University Press
CARBONDALE AND EDWARDSVILLE

LIBRARY OF CONGRESS CATALOGING IN PUBLICATION DATA

Narula, Uma, 1933–
    Development as communication.

    Bibliography: p.
    Includes index.
    1. Communication in economic development—India.
2. India—Economic policy—1947–   . I. Pearce, W.
Barnett.   II. Title.
HD76.N37   1985   338.954   85-2088
ISBN 0-8093-1223-9

Contents

FOUR
Indian Models of Development, 64

SEVEN

The Social Reality of the Masses,   152

EIGHT

The Interaction among Development Agents,   180

Figures

Preface

Studies of the "flow" of international news consistently show that particular places in the world are disproportionately under- or over-represented (Sreberny-Mohammadi 1984). For many years, India has been one of the "blank spaces" on the world map for many Americans, a mysterious place of which they seldom think and of which they even less frequently think realistically.

This unfortunate state of affairs was the case in 1982 when we were in India for the field work reported in this book. Since then, the situation has changed somewhat. Sensational news events and some significant entertainment programming have thrust India into the American awareness in a qualitatively different way. Even disembodied, aggregate "public opinion" has begun to deal with India as a modern democracy rather than— or at least as well as—a source of mystical religious teachers and an exotic background for Western adventures.

The earlier view still persists, of course. It was expressed in two popular films released while we were analyzing data. *Indiana Jones and the Temple of Doom* was set in the historical period of the 1930s. It portrayed India as a backward, superstitious, British colony which needed a (Western) hero to save a village, free enslaved children, overthrow an evil maharajah, and return magical stones to their rightful place in the village. Whatever its other values, it did not contribute to an understanding of India. Nor, we suppose, was it meant to. *Octopussy* was set in the present, and used India as the latest in a series of exotic settings for the exploits of James Bond, significantly a British government agent. Although some of the street scenes were realistic, no attempt was made to depict the modern social or political structure of the nation.

It takes only the slightest touch of cynicism to see these movies as expressing the same old colonial mentality against which Indians fought so hard and resourcefully.

A different attitude, one which accepts India as a viable, modern state with its own agenda and its own history, guided the film *Gandhi*. *Gandhi* was an unlikely commercial success because it dealt with the life and work of a non-Westerner and—more importantly—one who was not sumptuously dressed, who did not command vast armies or wealth, whose life was not filled with scandalous sexual passions, and who did not make a career that in any way contributed to the aid or comfort of the West.

Three other films, *The Far Pavilions*, *The Jewel in the Crown*, and *Passage to India*, focused on the troubled relationship between India and the West, personified in a romantic (or at least sexual) interracial relationship. In each case, the culture and modern history of India was an integral part of the story, rather than the geography and exotic customs merely providing a backdrop for Western adventurism.

Practically coinciding with the debut of the last two films, the Western press was filled with four major stories from India, each of which required recognition of India as a unique, independent, modern state.

The military action at the Golden Temple of Amritsar stunned and fascinated the United States. Freedom of religion is a constitutional right in both countries, but in the United States traditional definitions of this freedom have recently been strained by the political activism the New Christian Right and by outrage at the capture of the American embassy in Tehran by groups whose primary identification was as Muslims. Many Americans were fascinated, for reasons they might not care to admit, with the unfolding saga of how a democratic government might deal with militant religious groups.

The assassination of Prime Minister Indira Gandhi was stunning, unexpected, unsettling, and all too familiar in the long and recent history of politics in the United States. It was also uncannily similar to the first and final scenes in the movie *Gandhi*.

The tragedy at Bhopal, where a plant belonging to an American company spilled a deadly poison into the night sky, killing more than two thousand people, was not only "newsworthy" but showed many Americans a dimension of the relationship between the two countries of which they were unaware.

Finally, the political triumph of Rajiv Gandhi, seen festooned with flowers in streets filled with celebrating young adults, conveyed a message of patriotism to the United States, which itself is experiencing a renaissance of national pride. It also provided the "happy ending" for the year's events which American storytelling forms have led us to expect.

Before November of 1984, most Americans probably were unaware that Union Carbide had a plant in Bhopal, and if informed, probably would have found little to criticize. After the tragedy, of course, recriminations were received from every quarter. But the accusations about lax safety procedures at the plant, and of inadequate zoning regulations in the city, do not address the larger and more enduring question of international economic exploitation.

"Transnational corporations" are the current villains in the analyses of the global system of economic and political relations which seem to perpetuate and exacerbate gaps between the rich and the poor. In a simpler age, the villain was overt national colonialism.

This book tells a part of the story of one of humankind's oldest civilizations, improbably constituted as the world's largest democracy, as it strives to emerge from the residual effects of foreign domination to provide an acceptable quality of life for its citizens and to achieve an independent place within the international community. As a state, India's boundaries were formed by a combination of colonial policy and internal strife leading to the partition that created Pakistan and Bangladesh. There are many "nations" within the state, many religions, many cultures. One of the tasks of the government has been to create, from the many, one entity. It faces issues common to most of the new states created after the postwar breakups of the European empires: it pledged itself to democratic practices without a national consensus, and it pledged itself to achieve ambitious goals of social welfare. The combination of these pledges is troublesome: the first limits the government's autonomy; the second sets high standards by which its performance is evaluated.

This book is the story of communication. It describes the sometimes fumbling, sincere, often counterproductive attempts of many peoples to become a modern state without losing their distinctive traditions; of a stratified caste society pledged to democracy and equality; and of a strong central government attempting to engender initiative and responsibility by the masses.

It is the story of "development," the deliberate attempt to reduce the discrepancy between conditions of the rich and the poor. In India and elsewhere, development is one of the most pressing items on the agenda of humankind, equally relevant for wealthy nations such as the United States as for the less fortunate. Quite simply, by its very prosperity compared to other nations, the United States creates a condition which defines humankind as inequitably favored and sets into motion forces it neither intended nor necessarily recognizes. These forces will shape and guide our future as surely, and perhaps as ruthlessly, as will the invention of new technologies.

Lem (1983, 177–78) argues eloquently that the existing economic inequalities preclude attaining any society in which inequality has been eliminated. Setting his narrator in a future time in which he looks back on what is for us the present, he claims that inequality itself stifles the imagination of alternative social orders.

A civilization as "spread out" techno-economically as ours, with the front lines swimming in wealth and the rear guard dying of hunger, had by that very spread already been given a direction of future development. First, the troops behind would attempt to catch up with the leaders in material wealth, which, only because it had not yet been attained, would appear to justify the effort of that pursuit; and, in turn, the prosperous vanguard, being an object of envy and competition, would thereby be confirmed in its own value. If others imitated it, then obviously what it did must be not only good, but positively wonderful! The process thus became circular, since a positive feedback loop of motivation resulted, increasing the motion forward, which was spurred on, in addition, by the jabs of political antagonisms.

And further: a circle would result because it was difficult to come up with new solutions when the given problem already possessed some solutions. The United States, regardless of the bad that could be said of it, undoubtedly existed—with its highways, heated swimming pools, supermarkets, and everything else that gleamed. Even if one could think up an entirely different kind of felicity and prosperity, this could still only be, surely, in the context of a civilization that was both heterogeneous and—overall—not poor. But a civilization that reached a state of such equality and thereby became homogeneous was something completely unknown to us. It would be a civilization that had managed to satisfy the basic biological needs of all its members; only then, in its national sectors, would it be possible to take up the search for further, more varied roads to the future, a future now liberated from economic constraints. And yet we knew, for a certainty, that when the first emissaries of Earth went walking among the planets, Earth's other sons would be dreaming not about such expeditions but about a piece of bread.

The government of India has been impressed by arguments less pessimistic than Lem's, which claim that social justice not only *must* but *can* be achieved. They have not permitted their imaginations of a better society to be limited by the legacies of colonial exploitation, by their own history of feudalism, or by the examples of other nations. This is their story, and it is ours.

ACKNOWLEDGMENTS

The Indian Institute of Mass Communication and the Department of Communication at the University of Massachusetts contributed to this research by granting leaves to the authors, enabling them to travel between India and the United States. They also provided a hospitable environment in which to work. The Vivik Soni contributed the art work for many of the figures.

DEVELOPMENT AS COMMUNICATION

ONE

Introduction

DEVELOPMENT has been studied countless times from many perspectives. Many of these studies have focused on communication: as a useful tool for publicizing development plans, as the means by which exploitative social structures are perpetuated, or as the means of initiating sweeping cultural changes.

The research on which this book is based is unusual (if not unique) in that it envisions development *as* a form of communication, not as a political or economic process which includes communication as a more or less important component; we take a "communication perspective" on development. This leads us to analyze the interaction among the planners, change agents, and masses in two segments of Indian society.

The results of this analysis include several hypotheses offered as explanations of the history and current status of development in India: a "charmed loop" of perpetual obligation by planners, a distrust dilemma and a dependency dilemma for change agents, and learned dependency for the masses. We argue that the combination of these features is an unwanted, repeating pattern that is perpetuated by well-intentioned attempts by each of these development agents to change it. We conclude with some specific recommendations for breaking the pattern and allowing the "logic" of the interaction among these agents to continue to evolve.

We became interested in development through quite different but equally circuitous routes. When the Indian Institute of Mass

1

Communication (IIMC) was established in 1967, Narula was a Research Officer with the Research Council of the India International Center, and had been doing social and behavioral research on a number of topics. She accepted appointment to an equivalent position in the IIMC, and in this capacity was involved in many studies of Indian life and society.

Narula found the results of these studies puzzling. The current theories of how development worked and the role of communication in development (described in chapter 4) led to the happy expectation that the government's efforts would quickly be followed by self-sustaining social and economic progress. However, data indicated that this spontaneously regenerating development was not occurring, and she wondered why. She became interested in the "new paradigm" of development (described in chapter 3) that emphasizes "participation." Specifically, she wondered if the communication strategies used by the government had satiated the interests of the masses, and if the differing social structures in rural and urban communities affected the extent to which people became actively involved in development.

Pearce had been one of the louder (if not more profound) participants in "the great metatheory debate" of the mid–1970s that raged in scholarly circles in the United States. Existing concepts, descriptions, models, and prose accounts of the way communication works seemed unsatisfactory for several reasons, not least that the criteria by which any of these should be thought to be a successful "theory" were themselves made the focus of controversy. In the latter part of the decade, he and Vernon E. Cronen advanced what they called "the theory of the coordinated management of meaning" (or simply CMM).

The first phase of the "coordinated management project" took the form of some twenty studies designed to demonstrate the utility of those concepts, and was published as *Communication, Action and Meaning: The Construction of Social Realities* (Pearce and Cronen, 1980). Two aspects of that phase of the project were singled out for criticism.

Most of the studies dealt with very small groups: a couple, a family, a department at a university with twenty faculty members. In fact, one critic gleefully noted that one of our studies had more authors than subjects!

Most of the studies dealt with issues that were important to members of those social settings but scarcely commanded the attention of persons not involved. For example, one of the studies from which we learned a great deal concerned the relationship between two persons whom we called "Dave" and "Jan." For years after, various colleagues would slyly ask (or guess) their "real" identities, as if the value of the study derived from the celebrity status of the subjects rather than the nature of their relationship.

Another study focused on "unwanted repetitive patterns" in interactions between particular people. We found that most interpersonal relationships include disliked patterns of disagreement, argument, or dependency. These patterns are well known to the people involved; they can predict their recurrence with considerable accuracy but feel helpless to avoid them. This finding poses an intriguing theoretical issue. If people are at least partly rational and/or learn from their experience to avoid pain and seek pleasure, why do they get embroiled repeatedly in unwanted patterns? Despite the theoretical issue involved, however, most readers seemed to respond to the study on the basis of the forms of communication with which it dealt: arguments between spouses, disagreements with colleagues, etcetera. Our findings were cited more prominently in *Glamour* magazine than in scholarly journals.

The second phase of the "coordinated management project" was designed to apply its concepts to topics larger in scope than the small-group studies and to topics with greater intrinsic interest. It was about this time that Pearce and Narula met, when she began work toward a doctorate in the Department of Communication Studies at the University of Massachusetts.

The fit between this theory of communication and the topic of national development was far from immediately apparent. But as we began to learn from each other's work and to plan Narula's dissertation, we began to be more and more convinced that some important aspects of development were "invisible" to researchers and practitioners because of the concepts of communication they were using.

This observation is both general and specific. As a general principle, we see "blindness" as a necessary and inherent aspect of any set of concepts used to comprehend any set of phenomena. Theories are "terministic screens" which both illumine and mask various aspects of what is seen through them. Without a theory, our vision would be too dim to be very useful, but whatever theory we use imposes its own particular blinders. The specific set of blinders imposed by the concept of communication used by development officials in India initiated a very particular, counterproductive pattern of interaction between the government and the masses.

Narula's (1983) study of rural (village) and rurban (urban resettlement colony) communities focused on development awareness, motivation, and participation. Some of the results were startling. First, she found that the masses who were most aware of development issues and most discontented were least motivated to participate actively in development programs. Second, the success of development programs was not commensurate with the effort the government had expended and did not match the performance expected from contemporary theories of development.

We interpreted these findings as evidence that the masses had acquired a "learned dependency" on the government. Ironically, learned dependency precludes the success of development efforts, but is a consequence (unintended and unwanted) of the government's communication activities. We wondered why the masses developed learned dependency rather than engaged in active participation. Who was to blame?

Our search for an answer led us rather far afield. We finally concluded that the question was posed wrongly. The masses' learned dependency was not so much a *product* of their own or others' behavior as part of a *pattern* of interaction. The dilemmas and "charmed loop" of the change agents and planners are equivalent parts of the interaction, equally distressing and equally an impediment to achieving the objectives of development.

The government's development effort included a variety of actions: legislation that redistributed wealth and land; the creation of an immense, labor-intensive, conspicuous bureaucracy for the administration of development projects; the production and distribution of messages in a program designed to "inform, educate and communicate" (IEC) about development. Because it understood communication to be equated with messages, the government perceived only the IEC program as "communication."

Communication is generally thought of as a subset of human action. Speaking, listening to radio programs, and broadcasting educational programs over satellite-relayed television are instances of communication, but building a dam, prosecuting an exploitative landlord, or hiring a large staff for a government program are not. But this distinction cannot withstand careful scrutiny. A preferable way of thinking is to see communication as a potential aspect of any form of human activity; persons (or governments) may communicate by performing—or not performing—any particular action.

From this "communication perspective," all of the actions taken by the government—legislation, public works, and the development bureaucracy itself as well as the IEC program—are powerful forms of communication. Further, the land reform and building projects undertaken by the government conveyed a very different message than that of the interpersonal and mass-mediated IEC programs. The IEC programs declared that development required initiative from the grassroots, that the masses deserved a better life and could have it if they would act in particular ways. The legislation, public works, and bureaucracy, on the other hand, expressed the government's intention to take the responsibility for development, and disrupted the local community social structures that—in the best of cases—would have provided the mechanism for local initiative.

Caught between contradictory messages, the masses responded by waiting for the government to do development for them. Because the government thought of only their IEC activ-ities as communication, officials interpreted the masses as lazy or uncooperative, and designed more IEC programs with the same motif, reiterating the message that the masses had to show initiative. These programs were only part of a larger communi-cative context, however, and primarily increased the masses' confusion.

Our analysis focused on a reciprocal pattern of misperception and inadvertent communication in the interaction among plan-ners, change agents, and the masses. The theory of the coordi-nated management of meaning provides a useful terministic screen with which to describe the interaction of multiple agents through time, in which the pattern of interaction is not neces-sarily the same as the intentions of any of the agents involved. The result is the work reported in this book. We think it makes a number of contributions of interest to communication theo-rists (whether or not they are involved in development), to de-velopment planners and practitioners (whether or not they are involved in India), and to those interested in India (particularly those involved in the Indian development effort).

The concepts of "development" and "communication" have themselves developed in their meaning and use by the scholarly and professional communities. Among other things, communi-cation is now seen as a much more subtle, complex process than it had originally been thought, and much more basic to the pro-cess of development than had been realized. In fact, the earliest notions of development envisioned communication as an impor-tant tool for achieving other purposes but clearly as only a small component of a total development package. We review some of this "development of development" in chapter 3, and introduce a "communication perspective" that boldly reverses the initially proposed relationship between these concepts. Development, we argue, is a special case of communication processes.

Using this communication perspective, we present (in chapter 4) a rereading of the history of development efforts in India. Indian development planners have always been aware of but not slavish followers of the opinions of the "international develop-ment community"; indeed, the history of development in India includes some unique aspects. This reading shows an inherent tension between the objectives of socialism and of democracy in the context of economic stress, but notes that the Indian government has tenaciously pursued both.

In chapters 5, 6, and 7, using public documents and interviews as data, we describe the social realities and communication activities of planners and change agents; using an original study of two segments of Indian society as data, we describe the social realities and communication activities of the masses. Among other things, the latter data include new information about the communication networks within a progressive village and a rurban (urban slum with predominantly rural migrants as residents) colony. These networks explain some otherwise difficult-to-understand aspects of the masses' response to the government's IEC programs. Futher, we show how the agents in Indian development all have some form of "disorder" in their social realities, disorder that accounts for a pervasive discontent with development.

Finally, for discovering the hierarchical layering of meanings within social realities, we used an interpretive procedure we call "context analysis." This technique assumes that all interpretations and actions occur in context, and it seeks to identify the particular contexts that framed the interpretations and actions of a specific group of actors. In addition, we assume that some of the important contexts a person uses to make sense of the world include a concept of self, of other, of particular activities, and of institutions (Pearce and Cronen, 1980, chapter 5).

In chapter 8, we describe the interaction of planners, change agents, and masses. The analysis in this chapter assumes that the interaction among agents is a nonsummative combination of the intentions, interpretations, and actions of each participant, and shows how the pattern of interaction is dissimilar from the social realities of each of the agents involved in it. The sequence of acts often takes on a logic of its own that is different from the intentions of any agent.

In the final chapter, we reflect, from a communication perspective, on the results of the analysis. For example, the data suggest that "more" use of mass media in an IEC effort may be counterproductive. On this basis, we propose "dialogue action strategies," coupled with specific recommendations about handling discontent and dependency, for Indian development planners and the international development community. These strategies, and the analysis upon which they are based may be seen as the first major product of the second phase of the "coordinated management project."

TWO

Development, Communication, and India

ALTHOUGH THE PHYSICAL CHARACTERISTICS of the world have
changed very little during recorded history, social and political
geography is much more volatile. During the last 100 years,
historic monarchies of Europe and Asia have been demolished
or disempowered to the status of national symbols. The great
European colonial systems have broken up, and global power
has shifted away from Europe to two superpowers. One of the
most auspicious developments to occur in the last 50 years alone
is the establishment of more than 100 new nations, some of
which comprise what has come to be known as the "third world."

Most of these new nations are former colonies with a keen
sense of their new independence and of their history as victims
of international exploitation. Most are economically underdeveloped, many feel themselves relatively powerless in international economic and political struggles, and virtually all are
deeply suspicious of the motives of the industrialized nations.

Politics and economics are always intertwined, and the third
world is defined by both. Economically, the third world comprises those nations whose gross national product and per capita
income fall below the standard set by the industrialized nations.
Politically, the third world comprises those nations who have
made a deliberate decision to remain nonaligned in the struggle
between capitalist/democratic West and communist East.

One of the most distinctive features of this period is that the
industrialized nations have deliberately engaged in policies designed to stimulate economic and social progress in the under-

9

developed nations. Nations have always varied in resources, in industry, and in standards of living. To an unprecedented extent, in the last half century these differences have been made explicit, identified as a problem, and subjected to well-financed programs designed to eliminate—or at least reduce—them.

Periods of rapid change are valuable for learning about ourselves, and the social and political turbulence of the past half century have contained the stuff of which many lessons might be made. It has been particularly instructive about the means and limits of our ability to plan for growth, to undertake broad programs, and to act in a deliberate and effective manner to improve the quality of life for a rapidly expanding global population.

In the study of humankind, it does not often happen that a theory or program is decisively, conclusively shown to be right or wrong. The international effort to develop the underdeveloped countries of the third world—for whatever humanitarian or political reason motivated the effort—is such an instance. Development has elicited the interests and resources of a sufficient number of people and nations and has a clear enough criterion for success to permit a test of theories and an evaluation of programs.

Much of what has been learned has surprised and disappointed the authorities. The original notion of how development worked, the so-called "dominant paradigm," is clearly wrong, and has been judged so by most of those who originally constructed it. There is less agreement about what should replace the dominant paradigm than that it must be abandoned. In fact, there is an exciting and sometimes heated controversy about how development really works and about the role communication has in it.

The balance of this chapter addresses three questions. Why "development"? Why "communication"? And why "India"?

WHY DEVELOPMENT?

Since achieving independence in 1947, the government of India has made a concerted effort to meet the physical needs and improve the quality of life of the people and to strengthen the national economy. The commitment to national development was a bold step for a newly formed government confronting the instabilities of postwar international economics and the necessity to initiate a wide range of domestic policies. The concept of development itself required the government to take a novel role in Indian life, with unprecedented forms of contact between the central government and local communities. The government decided that it would pursue modernity aggressively, but it would do so using methods and materials of its own devising, adapted to the specific characteristics of Indian society.

The decision to tailor its development effort to the characteristics of its society and to experiment with various models of development contradicted the prevailing climate of opinion. After the Second World War, an "international development community" emerged that took as its mandate the modernization of underdeveloped countries and as its method a particular model of how development occurs.

There were several motivations for this historically unprecedented attempt to improve the fortunes of nations that did not enjoy the benefits of modern, industrial society. One motivation was the global/political concern for creating a lasting peace. The bitter lessons of the Treaty of Versailles (which did not so much "end" World War I as guarantee that it would be continued) led the victorious Allies of World War II to help rebuild the economies of the nations that had suffered the most direct damage from the fighting. The specific targets of this economic aid were the defeated nations, but the idea naturally spread to other nations whose economic infrastructure had been destroyed by combat operations and to those who had never developed an industrial economy.

A second motivation was humanitarian. Among other things, the war had made the peoples of the world conscious of each other and of their interdependence. The economic and social disparity among nations became very apparent. The United Nations was established with an explicit mandate to alleviate the causes of war, and identified these as including exploitation and relative deprivation. Delegates from the third world used the

11

United Nations and other forums to express their needs and to request assistance in economic development. Many called for the creation of a "New World Economic Order."

The third motivation involved the self-interest of the business leaders in the industrialized nations, who provided a surprisingly receptive audience for requests for development assistance. Industrialized nations need markets for their products, and even a populous country with a subsistence economy provides little opportunity for profits. For example, despite a major effort during the last part of the 19th and early 20th century, American businessmen had been unable to make the kinds of profits in China that they thought they should, in part because they could not use sophisticated technological goods and because most Chinese had little or no disposable income. To "invest" some funds in developing the economies of the third world seemed a sound business decision. The fact that this decision could also appear as humanitarian was no detriment.

The agenda of social scientists comprised a fourth motivation for international efforts in development. The comparative study of societies had really only begun in the half century before World War II, and social scientists were raising a series of questions directly related to development. For example, they wanted to know the mechanisms by which societies perpetuate themselves and are sometimes changed, and why some societies are so much more developed than others. Given other philosophical foundations for "doing" social science, this capable and energetic community might well have turned to historical, ethnographic, or critical studies. However, for good or ill, the philosophical position which they shared channeled them into projects of designing and assessing the effects of "planned change."

Quite without unconscionable collusion, the scientists became the perfect accessories of businessmen. The activities, if not interests, of businessmen paralleled that both of the governments of the victorious industrialized nations who wanted a lasting peace, and the governments of the underdeveloped countries who—newly enfranchised in the United Nations and strongly cognizant of the economic disparities among nations—wanted to share in the international affluence.

The "international development community" designates an unofficial consortium of persons who knew each other, regularly met at international conferences, shared a common "paradigm" about development, and managed an enormous amount of funds and labor. Their common and specific interests provided a distinctive—and, we now know, inaccurate—concept of development. They measured development with aggregate economic indicators, and envisioned it as a uniform process with only relatively minor local variations, repeating the sequence of steps taken by the Western industrialized nations. The pace of development could be quickened or slowed—but not fundamentally changed—by various programs of investing capital in industry and persuading individuals to adopt more "modern" attitudes.

A particular reading of both history and the philosophy of science supported the assumption that development follows a uniform sequence of stages and universally responds to standardized procedures for planned change. Social scientists defined their work as producing "law-like generalizations" of observable "regularities" in social structure and change. This perspective implied that an orderly pattern existed which was described with more or less accuracy by various generalizations, and legitimated an "activist" procedure of intervening in the process so as to produce and then measure the effects of various strategies. Further, the "economic miracle" of the postwar recovery of Japan and Germany seemed proof that the techniques for development were effective. Some have even suggested that the notion of a uniform process requiring massive transfers of funds and technology from the industrialized to the developing nations was appealing in part because it could be "sold" to the more industrialized countries and would in effect reverse some of the patterns of exploitation that occurred in colonial times.

The programs endorsed by this community naturally took an international focus. The forums in which development planning and funding took place were multinational. Representatives to these agencies from developing nations found common cause with each other based on a similar stance vis-à-vis the industrialized nations, which must have appeared to them as if they were involved in similar developmental processes. Given the "dominant paradigm" of how development worked, it only made sense to abstract from a variety of specific programs those procedures most effective in producing development.

One of the most endearing virtues of the international development community was its willingness to learn, and its dedicated search for data indeed tested its beliefs. One thing it learned was that there is no universal model for development, and that the local social structure is not just an obstacle to be overcome for modernization to occur but is the context from which development activities derive their meaning and significance. This learning led to the abandonment of the "dominant paradigm" in favor of other models (described in chapter 3).

WHY COMMUNICATION?

It has always been clear that communication is deeply implicated in the process of development. Early development experts were quite confident that they knew how communication works and what its role is in development. In India, early documents referred to communication as "plan publicity": a linear process of moving information from the government to the masses.

This confidence has evaporated. Both development and communication theorists tried for over fifteen years to devise an acceptable, useful model of communication. This effort, which Pearce (1985) called "the great model hunt," was futile. The modelers discovered that whatever communication was, it was not linear, and they ultimately abandoned the effort to achieve a satisfactory model. In addition, the notion of development itself has been questioned. It used to be thought of as something that can be measured by national economic indicators. Now many argue that these are insufficient—if not fundamentally misleading—criteria.

Chapter 3 reviews two paradigms of development and communication, and variations within each, that offer pictures of the way communication works. The first paradigm views develop-

ment as national industrialization and individual modernization; communication is seen as a movement of information from
one person or group to another with some effect. The second
paradigm views development as a complex structure of international economics and power relationships; communication as
a component of that structure perpetuates it. In our judgment,
neither of these paradigms is fully adequate. We present what
we call a "communication perspective" as an alternative to these
frames for thinking about development. This perspective views
development as the construction of a particular set of relationships, roles, and patterns of actions, and communication as the
process by which these are created.

WHY INDIA?

In chapter 4, we describe the history of development and communication efforts in India, and in the following chapters report
a study of development in India. There are three reasons, each
sufficient, for focusing on India.

First, a study of development has to focus somewhere. One of
the things we have learned is that development is particular
rather than general; it reflects the specific social, cultural, and
economic factors of a particular place rather than being a time-
less process occurring pretty much the same way everywhere.

It is this emphasis on the particularity of development that
makes specific studies of given communities essential. To be
sure, there are general principles which can be abstracted from
studies of development in general, and these can "edify" development theorists and planners; and the procedures of analysis
used in the present study can be applied to any given case. But
there can be no "expert" on development who is not an expert
on development in some particular place and time. Development in democratic India, for example, is not the same as development in Marxist countries, such as Cuba and China, that
have no comparable commitments to individual liberty and self-
determination. Further, there are differences in the process of
development based on the specifics of the program and the
structure of the community even within a country.

The nature of development expertise is necessarily tied to specifics, and to the meaning of specific events and objects in an emerging sequence of actions by the various agents involved in development. The course of this interaction itself can make either a "problem" or a "solution" out of a "situation." Stories about specific development problems—e.g., the dirty latrines in the rurban community of Jhangirpuri and the stagnant pond outside the village of Lampur—may seem far removed from the conference rooms of the United Nations or the the offices of the World Bank or the classrooms of the University of Massachusetts, or even from government buildings in Delhi. From the perspective of the dominant paradigm, the Jhangirpuri latrines or the Lampur pond would be of interest only to the extent that they bear on a generalization about development, for instance, as an exemplar of the general process or as an anomaly that challenges the accuracy of a generalization. But the dominant paradigm has "passed" (Rogers, 1976), and we now know that the process of development occurs in ways not trivially influenced by the details of the specific local community.

This line of reasoning seemingly forces us into the undesirable position of arguing that every specific instance of development must be understood on its own grounds, with no possiblity of general knowledge. We do interpret the data collected under the dominant paradigm as suggesting that "empirical generalizations" about a uniform process of development are not a valid or even most desirable form of knowledge, but this does not lead to a thorough-going relativism. One purpose of this book is to say something useful about development in two specific localities; another is to present a "communication perspective" that facilitates analysis of any given development program or community.

The application of this perspective gives the development "expert," or a participant in the development program, the capacity to understand various aspects of the process in greater depth. It confers something closer to "wisdom" than to "knowledge," a procedure for detecting and assessing the importance of particular features of the local scene rather than "law-like statements" that describe a context-free process of development. "Expertise" in development derives less from a well-practiced array of procedures or from a set of generalizations to apply to all occasions than from a way of working oneself into an analysis of the specific social context and of assessing the relative importance of various aspects of particular details of the development program.

The second reason for our focusing on India is that development is particularly important for India, because India is now the second largest nation on earth (one out of eight human beings at this moment is Indian), and demographic projections suggest that by the middle of the next century it will have the largest population of any nation. The sum total of human misery or satisfaction, the potential for achievement or lost opportunities, is magnified by the sheer size of India's population. Development is also important for India because it is a socialist democracy, whose government has pledged to improve the lot of the people and that regularly submits itself to the vote of the people. India is a secular, nonaligned democracy whose domestic viability depends, at some level at least, on the consent of the governed; and this consent is explicitly based on the government's ability to bring about a better standard of living for all concerned.

Finally, development in India is interesting. India has always refrained from being overly influenced by the opinions of the "international experts" in development. While the development programs in India have borrowed from the concepts and practices developed elsewhere, they have never simply reflected the international development community. In part, this is due to the influence of Mahatma Gandhi, who provided an early "meta-model" for development; and in part it reflects a willingness of Indian planners to learn from and utilize their own history in development efforts.

Also, India has made major and innovative commitments to the development program. It has been the leader among third world nations in the use of satellite technology as a means of development, and it has invested in a huge infrastructure of change agents who work in "blocks" in rural areas.

Further, development in India presents a puzzling anomaly.

The program has unquestionably been successful, but the predominant reaction from virtually all those involved—planners, change agents and masses—is discontent. Consider two examples.

The Latrines of Jhangirpuri

Jhangirpuri is an urban resettlement colony. It was built by the Delhi Development Authority (DDA) as a way of providing basic amenities to some of the thousands of persons who have migrated to the urban area from villages all across the country. The basic structures consist of housing lanes of one-room tenements.

A block of ten public latrines are provided for every ten housing lanes (containing a hundred houses). The DDA hires some of the residents who are sweepers by caste to clean the latrines as well as to remove garbage from the colony.

The residents of Jhangirpuri are of several castes, including the harijans. The term "harijan" was coined by Gandhi over thirty years ago for sweepers, who were treated literally as untouchables. It means "children of God," and was part of Gandhi's effort to raise the social status of this caste. Since then, social education as well as legislation has been used by the government to uplift harijans. As a result, this class has a much greater awareness of its rights. However, even now only they work as sweepers.

The latrines are chronically filthy. The residents, very dissatisfied, complain to the DDA official that the sweepers do not clean the latrines or remove the garbage from the colony. They make it clear that they feel the DDA is inefficient in administering this aspect of the development project.

The DDA officials complain that they have done all anyone could expect. They have hired a sufficient number of sweepers to keep the latrines and the colony clean. When confronted with the fact that the people they have hired are not working, the DDA officers admit that the sweepers would rather gossip than work, but explain that they cannot fire them because they will take violent actions.

One aspect of the problem is the new consciousness of social status among the harijans. They are not willing to work as sweepers for people with the same economic status. They do not mind working for the higher castes, but they do not want to work for the poor lower castes.

The latrines remain filthy, but there is a welter of reciprocated blame. The administrators blame their harijan employees, who have agreed to accept employment but then refused to perform their tasks and finally engaged in disruptive acts to prevent the administrators from firing them and hiring others. The residents blame both the harijans as a class and the administrators. They see the harijans as irresponsible and the administrators as inept in making their employees work. The harijans blame the social structure that expects them to perform menial functions that serve persons of their own economic class.

And the latrines remain dirty.

The Pond Outside Lampur

Outside Lampur, there is a pond into which the sullage from the village drains. The land around Lampur is quite level, so the flow of water is very slow.

Before development programs reached Lampur, the people, not understanding community hygiene, were unaware that the pond constituted a threat through polluted water and as a breeding ground for malaria-carrying mosquitoes. Two of the goals of development were to make the people aware of health hazards posed by the pond and to desire change. These goals have been achieved. The people now attribute their stomach problems to the polluted water, and they fear malaria. For more than ten years, they have complained to the government that something should be done about the pond. On several occasions, the headman has even gone to Delhi to present the village's demands.

The villagers, very dissatisfied with the government's failure to respond, feel they have contracted in good faith with the government for development but have been let down. Local government officials say the villagers are poorly informed. The pond is necessary for sewage drainage and now presents no immediate health hazard. The government regularly sprays it to control mosquito breeding, and has provided tube wells as an alternative source for drinking water. There appears to be a blockage in the communication networks. The top-down channels that alerted the villagers to the problem worked, as did the bottom-up channel by which the villagers expressed their discontent. But the government's "feedback" to the "feedback" provided by the villagers does not get through, making the villagers feel unheard, ineffective, and imperilled.

Higher levels of government officials say there is a better, longer-lasting way of alleviating the health hazard posed by the pond, which the local change agents apparently do not know. This indicates a second blockage of communication, this time within the development bureaucracy.

Meanwhile, the people of Lampur worry and complain, and feel excluded from the process of development.

DEVELOPMENT SUCCESS AND ITS DISCONTENTS

A number of observations can be made about development in these communities. The development effort has been successful on several counts. The pond outside Lampur is a "fact," and has existed for a very long time. That it is perceived as a "problem" reflects the success of the government in informing the people about health hazards; that they insistently demand something be done about it evidences the success of the government in instilling a "modern" set of attitudes toward active redress of wrongs. The behaviors of the villagers is a far cry from what it was before the development effort began, when they were ignorant of the problem and fatalistically accepted whatever *is* as what it *should* be. Similarly, the latrines and the community of Jhangirpuri itself exist only because the government's commitment to development included building urban resettlement colonies. The quality of life for the residents of Jhangirpuri is better than it would have been if the government had not acted.

Another observation is that all the participants in development seem discontented: frustrated by the pace of development, convinced of the failures of other agents, constrained by the shortcomings of others. How should we think about this pervasive discontent?

Pervasive discontent surprised those involved in development efforts, but it is not hard to understand it from the perspective of a greater distance. In fact, there are all too many (perhaps too easy) explanations. Those taking a "social exchange" perspective see discontent as "the revolution of rising expectations" which is a natural concomitant of social and economic improvement. Abraham Maslow's (1971) motivation theory suggests that people always "grumble"; it urges planners and managers to be unconcerned about the occurrence of grumbling as long as they pay some attention to the content of those grumbles. Others advance a "cultural personality" theory, explaining discontent as a form of culturally patterned and sanctioned behavior. Still others propose the explanation that persons who have adopted a "modern" set of attitudes are obviously frustrated by any set of circumstances that impede their swift accomplishment of objectives: the "dream deferred" is less satisfying than no dream at all.

Explanations of why there is so much discontent become important because actions are based on them. Hard-nosed pragmatists, concerned with the effects (especially the immediate and "objective" effects) of development, might disregard discontent entirely. If development programs are succeeding well enough according to objective indices of adoption, productivity, etcetera, then the attitudes of the people are unimportant.

There are two reasons for avoiding this sanguine "benign neglect" of discontent. The first is rather straightforward. If the masses have a bad attitude toward development, particularly if they define themselves as "consumers" rather than "participants" in development, there will be severe limits on the success of development projects. The government has all along realized that it can do only a limited amount of the work necessary to achieve development objectives, and thus development programs "succeed" only if they become self-sustaining. Not only must the masses adopt new products, they must become actively involved in development projects, contributing their own work and materials to maintain and supplement that which the government provides. Profound discontent has not led to that kind of involvement. Rather, the participation of the masses has been passive or dependent.

The second reason for paying attention to discontent is that it may mean far more than it seems. Rather than simply the expression of an attitude, we suggest that discontent is the expression of a particular type of "disordered social reality" produced by the communication among the planners, change agents and masses. All agents in this development dialogue find themselves in a situation in which they *must* act but have no available actions that *suffice*. Caught in some form of a "paradoxical injunction," the various agents have expressed their frustration as "discontent."

The deeper we explore this anomaly, the more interesting it gets. We conclude that the interaction among these agents has created social realities that are curiously convoluted, placing the agents in dilemmas such that nothing they can do or can have happen to them is seen "simply." For reasons which are grounded in the history of the interactions among these agents, everything has multiple meanings and evaluations. Some surprising things fall out of this analysis. For one, "more" communication, particularly more mass communication, will not appreciably change the situation. It is not simply that there is a "saturation" of information, but a more complex situation: the social realities of the masses provide a context in which mass mediated messages are treated in ways that preclude their having the desired effect.

THREE

Paradigms of Development

LIKE EVERY COMMUNITY with a shared mission, development theorists and practitioners work within the perspective provided by "paradigms." According to Kuhn (1970), paradigms have two components. The "disciplinary matrix" consists of clusters of assumptions, generalizations and value commitments, some of which may be unacknowledged. The "research exemplar" consists of sets of practices in which they participate. Among those who share a paradigm, it is easy to understand and be understood. Certain lines of action are highly predictable and seem clearly "right." If the paradigm is particularly robust, all the members of the community are likely to make identical judgments, or at least be easily persuaded to agree.

Again like other communities, in politics and the social sciences for instance, development theorists and practitioners are better described as a number of subcommunities, each acting out of overlapping, but still somewhat different, paradigms. The mission statments of each subcommunity might be similar, even identical; and all would endorse a common goal if stated at a sufficient level of generality and abstraction. However, within the common perspective, they operate with very different assumptions, practices, and values, and often take their differences as very important.

There have been three major approaches to understanding development, and we propose a fourth.

The predominant approach is what we call "modernization." This way of thinking about and doing development was historically the first and has been the framework in which most of the resources for development have been expended. There has been quite a bit of change within this perspective, however. Its spokespersons differentiate the earlier and the revised forms of this approach by calling them the "dominant paradigm" and the "new paradigm."

The assumption that development practitioners can and should promote modernization is strongly critiqued by those we identify by their commitment to "international equity." There are two variations of this paradigm, both of which focus on patterns of international relations. One is called the "interdependency model," the other the "dependency model."

The third group is identified by their awareness of poverty and their commitment to meet the basic needs of the world's poor people.

Finally, we introduce what we call the "communication perspective."

MODERNIZATION

The Dominant Paradigm

The paradigm that united the international development community in the 1950s and 1960s sought to explain and facilitate the transition from traditional to modern societies. It was based on a kind of international Calvinism that attributed poverty to some defect in the poor person—or, in this case, nation—and stood ready to "redeem" the sinner by exorcising that defect.

This paradigm was based on the observation that the differences in per capita income between developed and underdeveloped nations could not be explained in terms of differences in natural resources or other factors outside human control. Add to this a value structure that identified an absence of certain modern conveniences and material culture as a lamentable problem demanding redress, and the condition of most of the new nations was interpreted as a plight, caused by their own failure to use their human and natural resources to full potential. The problem might be due to a lack of technology, an inability to put natural resources to their best use, the lack of adequate economic institutions, or the inefficiency of government or market machinery. The solution was to change those human factors which inhibited full utilization of the resources. The developed nations of the West were taken as the ideal. In comparison, the less industrialized nations of Asia, Africa, and Latin America seemed economically impoverished and unable to control their environment or withstand unexpected emergencies. The nomenclature reveals the ideology. The new nations were categorized as "underdeveloped"; some theorists, a bit more sensitive to the stigma of being "backward," referred to them as "developing nations," a term whose cheery optimism was thought to ameliorate the presumptions embedded in it.

Development consisted of an attempt to increase productivity, economic growth, and industrialization by capital-intensive investments, sometimes tied to administrative reforms. The favorable effects of these innovations would "trickle down" from the elites throughout the society. In the process, the culture would be transformed from "traditional" to "modern." Every dimension of this transformation was perceived positively. Static, agricultural, primitive, rigid, and ascriptive societies were to be remade into dynamic, industrialized, urbanized, and socially mobile nations.

As usual, the features of the dominant paradigm are clearer in hindsight than they were at the time. It now appears there were two emphases within the dominant paradigm. The first originated in the equation of underdevelopment with poverty and lack of specific material products. From this perspective, the obvious way to alleviate underdevelopment was to make those nations more like the developed ones. This strategy led to programs of capital-intensive investment in industry and to assessments of development in terms of the Gross National Product (GNP), per capita income, and proportion of GNP in industrial products rather than in agriculture or raw materials.

The second emphasis derived from an analysis of the cultures of underdeveloped nations. Lerner, Inkeles and others noted

25

that the attitudes and folkways of traditional peoples are ill-suited for the demands of modern society, such as working in factories and participating in political units larger than the local community. From this perspective, a necessary complement to industrialization was "modernization," the planned change of values, attitudes and behaviors of individuals in developing countries.

Communication was seen as an indispensible tool for making the people of underdeveloped societies more modern. In a nutshell, the dominant paradigm envisioned communication as a flow of messages that traveled only one way, from top (the government) to bottom (the people)—a process of "conveying informative and persuasive messages from a government to the public in a downward, hierarchical way" (Rogers 1976, 133). Mass media channels, including broadcast technology when possible and change agents when not, were used to inform and persuade the people about development projects. The people were assigned the passive role of acquiescing to appeals for social change.

This simple—much too simple—concept of communication was accompanied by an uncritical faith in its power. Pye (1963, 3–4) attributed the "downfall of traditional society" to the pressure of communications. Lerner (1958) alluded to mass media as a "magic multiplier" for development efforts. Inkeles and Smith (1974, 146) concluded that the most powerful agents in the inculcation of individual modernization were the mass media, the school, and the factory. Schramm (1978) confessed that communication was often thought of as a "bullet" that hit a target with predictable effects. Specifically, these development strategists thought of communication (that is, the mass media) as "conveying" a commodity to the masses. Acquiring information and education as commodities, they thought, the masses would acquire more "modern" attitudes, adopt innovations, and participate in an increasingly industrialized economy.

LERNER'S COMMUNICATION MODEL FOR MODERNIZATION. Lerner (1958) identified development with modernization and social change. In his judgment, the underdeveloped countries could not exploit their resources because of the attitudes and practices that constituted "traditional" society. One of the first objectives of development programs was, therefore, to change individuals, making them "modern." With other dominant paradigm theorists, he developed an extensive list of characteristics that differentiated "traditional" and "modern" individuals. In Inkeles and Smith's (1974, 290) characterization, "Modern man is an informed participant citizen, has a marked sense of personal efficacy, is highly independent and autonomous, and is ready for new experiences and ideas."

Three major factors are required for inculcating modernity: media exposure, political participation, psychic empathy. Each is seen as antithetical to traditional, village culture. As shown in Figure 3.1, Lerner believed that "mass media exposure" was a key catalyst in the sequence leading toward modernization. In

Urbanization → Literacy → Economic and Political Participation

↖ ↗

Mass Media Exposure

Figure 3.1. Lerner's model of modernization.

development programs, the role of communication was to show "traditional" individuals that there was a world outside their experience, to enable them to relate to persons from diverse backgrounds, and to persuade them to adopt a particular set of beliefs and values that would facilitate their participation in the industrialized society being developed. By increasing mass media exposure, the "passing" of traditional society can be speeded.

ROGERS'S CONCEPT OF THE DIFFUSION OF INNOVATIONS. Rogers (1971, 10–11) focused more at the level of social systems than Lerner, although still taking the individual as the unit of analysis. He defined modernization as "the process by which individuals change from a traditional way of life to a more complex,

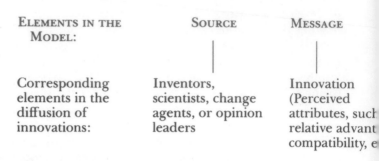

ELEMENTS IN THE MODEL:	SOURCE	MESSAGE
Corresponding elements in the diffusion of innovations:	Inventors, scientists, change agents, or opinion leaders	Innovation (Perceived attributes, such relative advant compatibility, e

Figure 3.2. Rogers's model of the diffusion of innovations (Rogers 1971).

technologically advanced, rapidly changing style of life," and development as "modernization of the social system."

His specific interest was the "diffusion" of innovations. Diffusion is a special form of communication in which some change agent confronts (in person or by means of some medium) the members of a social system with an innovation and persuades them to adopt it. Rogers (1971, 20) claimed that the diffusion process could be summarized by the SMCRE model, as shown in Figure 3.2. This model depicts a top-to-bottom linear process. Within this framework, only the "source" communicates actively and purposefully, and the problem posed to the source is that of finding a means by which "receivers" can effectively be induced to adopt the desired innovation.

Criticisms of the Dominant Paradigm

In the clarity of hindsight, the dominant paradigm is all too vulnerable to its critics. However, the criticisms have led to alter-

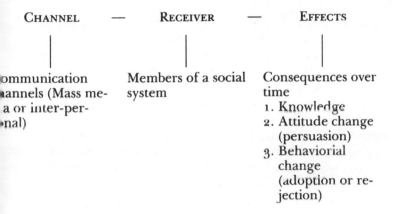

CHANNEL	—	RECEIVER	—	EFFECTS
ommunication annels (Mass me- a or inter-per- nal)		Members of a social system		Consequences over time 1. Knowledge 2. Attitude change (persuasion) 3. Behaviorial change (adoption or rejection)

native formulations of the nature of development—and of the role of communication in development.

PRAGMATIC CRITICISM. The most telling criticism of the dominant paradigm was that it had a fair test and failed. It failed as a guide for how to do development in many of the developing nations in the "free world." Assessments of the quality of life and of the differential between developed and developing nations show that very little was accomplished (Schramm and Lerner 1976). Further, it failed as a theory; it did not adequately explain development. A number of countries that have not followed the procedures outlined in the dominant paradigm have shown a great deal of development. The experiences of the People's Republics in China and in Cuba, as well as other nations, show that there are "multiple and varied models of development . . . now in style" (Rogers 1976, 133).

The pragmatic is the most telling criticism. If the dominant paradigm had succeeded as guide and explanation of development, other—more profound—criticisms would have received less attention.

ANALYTIC CRITICISM. The theorists of the dominant paradigm "blamed the victim," attributing the "cause" of underdevelopment to domestic factors. Bordenave (1974), Beltran (1976) and others argued that features in the social structure such as government bureaucracy, a top-heavy land tenure system, caste relationships, exploitative linkages, corruption, and political instability precluded successful industrialization. Lerner (1958), Schramm (1964) and others claimed that development efforts often failed because the individuals in traditional societies were resistant to change and did not have the appropriate attitudes and values to participate in an industrialized society.

The analysis of the social structure of underdeveloped nations by "dominant paradigm" strategists was superficial. In their attempt to describe a single path of development, they were insufficiently attentive to the differences between developing countries which had rich natural resources and those which did not, a feature that creates considerable differences in development dynamics. Further, the dominant paradigm did not take into account the economic vulnerability of developing nations in the international marketplace. Terms of trade between developed and developing nations often worked to perpetuate or exacerbate the economic differential between them. Industrialization often took the form of "branch plants" of international corporations, which made the economies of developing countries vulnerable to the fluctuations of markets far outside their sphere of influence, and many forms of technical assistance resulted in an increased dependency of the developing countries on their erstwhile benefactors.

In reverse, the world oil crises, for example, made some developing nations suddenly rich and displayed the dependency of the industrialized nations on imports of raw materials. At the very least, this challenged certain dominant paradigm assumptions, for instance, that the causes of underdevelopment were purely domestic.

IDEOLOGICAL CRITICISM. The dominant paradigm made an unquestioned assumption that change was good and progress the ideal—progress as defined by the Western industrial countries. But others found it possible to question this ideology.

Environmental pollution resulting from industrialization is a problem in developed countries and a rapidly increasing concern in developing countries. Confronted with the prospects of damage to the environment, some challenged the Western model of development as an ideal.

Overpopulation continues to diminish the economic gains made by development; it led many to wonder if unending growth was possible or desirable, and whether high technology was the most appropriate engine for development. Further, the benefits of development were being distributed inequitably, leading again to fundamental questions about the value of participating in development efforts.

Some Second Thoughts About Communication

One aspect of the explanatory failure of the dominant paradigm involves the alleged efficacy of mass mediated communication. For example, because many studies showed a high correlation between media exposure and adoption of innovations or development of attitudes associated with modernity, researchers under the influence of this paradigm attributed *causality* to these data, concluding that media exposure produced modernity. This interpretation is now seen as completely unwarranted. At the most, such data can indicate only the co-occurrence of phenomena, not a causal relationship, but one of the functions of a paradigmatic framework is to allow interpretations to go beyond the information given.

One illustration of this complex of interpretations was reported by Rogers (1976, 136): an anomaly that challenged the paradigmatic assumption of the power of communication. Despite the high correlation between modernity and media exposure, mass media were "almost never reported" when individuals who had adopted innovations were asked the sources or channels through which they learned about the new product or idea. They almost always cited communication with their peers, in what the dominant paradigm would call "bottom-bottom" communication patterns.

In the painful process of reinterpreting these studies and the paradigm which produced them, some researchers noted that little attention had been paid to the *content* of the messages in the mass media. The unsophisticated view of communication in the dominant paradigm simply did not lead to a more detailed analysis of particular communication events once it was noted that the messages had a prodevelopment flavor. When content analysis was done of development messages (e.g., Barghouti 1974), it was found that very little specific information was being provided. In better times, this finding would have harbored hope sufficient for the defense of the paradigm along these lines: The media have not had the effect we anticipated, but it is because the content of the messages broadcast has been deficient; we should not abandon the paradigm until more research has been done, including field experiments with better crafted messages. As it was, the disillusionment with the paradigm was too great to sustain such a defense.

The social structure of local communities in traditional societies was always assumed to be an obstacle to modernization, but one the mass media could overcome. It is widely thought that the development of the printing press was the deathknell of the feudal society in Europe. Books in medieval villages have been described as "gunpowder for the mind," expanding horizons of knowledge and subverting local patterns of authority. Much of the impetus for the development of literacy in third world countries, and for the spread of the broadcast media that do not require literacy, springs from a desire to have a comparable effect in twentieth-century underdeveloped countries. A number of studies, however, showed the relative intractability of the local social structure to the "top-down" communication efforts under the dominant paradigm (e.g., Grunig 1971).

These successive blows to their assumptions seriously, and understandably, eroded the confidence of dominant paradigm theorist and practitioners in how they thought about and engaged in development efforts. Alternatives to the dominant paradigm dealt with communication in quite different ways.

The New Paradigm

As previously indicated, the "modernization" approach to understanding development was basically divided into two emphases: the earlier phase, designated the "dominant paradigm"; the revised form, the "new paradigm".

The "new paradigm" shares the empiricist, activist orientation of the dominant paradigm, and was offered by many of the same persons who—to their credit—recognized the limitations of the model with which they were first identified. It differs from the dominant paradigm by attempting to expunge its Calvinistic evangelicalism and by having a radically different concept of both development and communication.

The new paradigm is actually a "metamodel" of development (Rogers 1976) with some distinctive commitments. Where the dominant paradigm assumed there is only one efficacious pathway to development, the new paradigm assumes that development can—and should—take a variety of forms. Which pathway is appropriate depends on a particular country's social, political, and economic structure, its development needs, and the availability of resources and technology. The dominant paradigm's monocular vision focuses on industrialization as the one sure route to development; the new paradigm has a less restrictive purview, encompassing labor-intensive technology, decentralization in planning, both domestic and international economic factors, and the characteristics of the local social structures.

Six features characterize the new paradigm's emphasis on particular social systems (Rogers 1976, 129). 1) Development objectives are stated in terms of improvements in the quality of life for individuals more than in macroeconomic goals of increases in GNP or tonnage of industrial exports. This shift of emphasis is based on an explicit recognition of the importance of maintaining a continuity with traditional lifestyles rather than simply importing the Western model of society and forcing indigenous peoples to adapt to it. The ideal development is envisioned as a

33

locally unique blending of modern and traditional values and institutions. 2) Planning and decision making are decentralized, eliciting popular participation at the local level. 3) Self-reliance, self-development and self-management are incorporated as development objectives as well as strategies. 4) "Distributive justice" of economic gains is sought so that inequities between rich and poor do not increase. Villagers and the urban poor are priority targets of development programs. Rather than wait for economic benefits to trickle down from affluent elites, socioeconomic gaps are reduced by bringing up the sector of the society that lags behind. 5) An emphasis is placed on "society specific" models of development communication. These models include "traditional media" and descriptions of the "communication networks" within the community. 6) Attention is given to social and international structural factors that impede development, rather than concentrating exclusively on deficiencies of individuals or of the nation.

Participation is the key characteristic of the new paradigm. In practice, this requires initiating novel forms of interaction among various groups within the society, itself a formidable task. The problem confronted by development theorists and practitioners was not only economic but social. How could they assess the implications of various forms of social interaction and devise means by which they could be implemented?

This task required a fundamental rethinking of many components of the "disciplinary matrix" of the "modernization" orientation. When the dominant paradigm was abandoned, the mechanistic perspective on communication went with it—that is, the process by which messages were transmitted from the "top" to the "bottom" of a vertical structure. The concept that communication was a neutral tool used to inform and influence people was revised, in part due to the activity of a large academic discipline organized for the study of communication in a wide variety of contexts. This discipline went through a series of changes roughly parallel to the development community. In each succeeding formulation, communication appeared more complex and its effects more subtle. In the new paradigm, development theorists began to think of communication as a process of social interaction through a balanced exchange of information. The emphasis on participation emerged not simply due to the dashed hopes of particular development efforts but as a failure of the whole philosophical orientation of the international development community that was expressed in the dominant paradigm.

PARTICIPATION AND COMMUNICATION. The climate of opinion in which the new paradigm was formed explicitly endorsed liberal and democratic values. The new approach stipulated that development programs should improve the quality of life for specific persons and that the planning and implementation of these programs should be carried out *with* the people rather than *for* them.

Within this framework, participation has dual value. It is, of course, a means to an end: producing plans, acquiring local information, implementing programs, etcetera. But it is at the same time the end itself. The participation of the poor who are often without an effective public voice has become a central concern in the policies of many development agencies. Academic advisors recommend involving the poor in the decisions that effect them, soliciting their contribution of resources to development activities, and assuring them they will in fact be the beneficiaries of adopting innovations. The value of development is not always self-evident to those people whose lifestyles are most likely to be affected by it, and participatory communication involves them in a process which increases the probability that they will not only "adopt" but use, repair, and care for the machinery and amenities they receive as part of development efforts.

Participatory communication also has a desirable effect on the people involved as well as facilitating the success of particular development programs. It confers a sort of political emancipation, a new awareness of one's economic and social condition (Ryan and Kaplun 1980). One scenario popular among new paradigm development theorists is that participation in development projects is an educational process that starts with an analysis of reality, follows with a rejection of the ideology of the elite

35

classes, and finally leads to motivation of the unprivileged population toward concerted action for social change. The new paradigm sees participatory communication as essential for development. Failure to engage all of the human resources in the task of development not only acts as a brake on the economic growth but does little to cure the basic causes of social and political instability that pose a constant threat to the gains being achieved on the economic front.

In the rush to extol the virtues of participation and incorporate it into development projects, there is, however, a disturbing fact; there is little agreement on what participation is or what its basic dimensions are. This problem is manifest in different forms: Definitions of participation are internally inconsistent; participation is often described very abstractly, thus producing ambiguity at more concrete levels; efforts to explain participation deal with its causes rather than its consequences. Finally, very few analyses of actual experiences with participatory approaches to development can be found, because too many studies simply assume participation is desirable and thus neglect empirical tests of that assumption.

The problems faced by new paradigm development theorists can be summarized in five questions:

1. What is participation, or what may usefully be regarded as participation in terms of development ends and means?

2. What are the most significant issues or dimensions associated with the analysis and support of participation in development?

3. To what extent should the analysis of participation treat it as an end—an objective in its own right—and to what extent as a means to other ends through the mobilization of resources, shared administrative burdens, etcetera?

4. To what extent should participation be viewed in relation to development projects and to what extent to the larger society?

5. To what extent should participation be regarded as something observable, and to what extent might attitudes or subjective factors be considered in the definition?

These questions can be answered in terms of three topics: the "what," "who," and "how" of participation. Cohen and Uphoff

(1976) identified four forms of participation: in decision making, in implementation, in benefits, in evaluation. Participation in the process of decision making implies accepting responsibility for identifying problems and choosing solutions. Participation in implementation consists of contributing resources, administering and coordinating projects, and enlisting in the project. Participation in the results of development programs may include features which can be interpreted as harmful as well as beneficial. Participation in evaluation refers to the process of assessing programs and giving feedback about their efficacy.

The Rural Development Committee (RDC) developed a taxonomy of participants and a taxonomy of form of participation. Who are—or might be—the participants involved in development? Participants range from foreign consultants to the residents of the local area. Development differs depending on who participates in the program.

The RDC taxonomy for participation includes the basis, form, extent, and effectiveness of participation. One important observation is Coombs's (1980) distinction between "passive" and "active" participation. Passive participation occurs, for instance, when local residents listen politely to messages in a top-down pattern and accept handouts but do not alter their customary views or behavior. "Active" participation occurs when a village organizes itself democratically to examine its needs and options to make decisions, mobilize its resources, and seek outside help when it needs it. Silberman (1979) described "functional participation" as that which occurs when the government manages to mobilize people for goals which the government sets. "Popular participation" occurs when people are engaged in programs of their own design and for their own goals.

The problems of implementing active or popular participation are formidable. For instance, existing social structures can facilitate or preclude participation. A society with little political or military stability is less conducive to planning and implementation of development programs than a calmer society, one in which the institutions are more dependable. Further, broad-based participation in planning and implementation is much

37

more likely to produce constructive, consensual projects in societies with shared traditions and common symbolic systems. However, much of the third world consists of "states" whose boundaries were formed as a result of colonial legacies and the aftermath of the Second World War; these states may include multiple "nations," each with its own language, cultural institutions, and ethnic bonds. Van Voos's (1979) analysis of Malaysia as a democracy without consensus is applicable to many other nations as well, certainly including India.

There is another difficulty which must be acknowledged: deliberate obstruction by the elites. Effective participation implies a basic transformation of communication and media policy, and in many societies could not be envisaged without some fundamental social changes. Any strongly vertical society, in which power and decision making are controlled by an elite, will not allow or not be affected by the kind of horizontal and bottom-up patterns of communication necessarily implied by the notion of participation. If such patterns occur, they are equivalent to a coup.

DIFFUSION THEORY REVISITED. Rogers was one of the theorists most responsive to the implications of the new paradigm. Consistent with what he and others had learned, he changed his mind about both development and communication. In 1971, he defined development as "modernization at the social system level" which occurs when "new ideas are introduced into a social system in order to produce higher per capita incomes and levels of living through more modern production methods and improved social organization" (Rogers, 1971, 11). In 1976, this definition had changed substantially. Development was seen as "a widely participatory process of social change in a society, intended to bring about both social and material advancement (including greater equality, freedom, and other valued qualities) for the majority of the people through their gaining greater control over their environment" (Rogers 1976).

Well aware that the diffusion model fit the dominant paradigm's focus on technology and on top-down communication, Rogers (1976, 138–43) recognized that the failure of the dominant paradigm implied the necessity to revise his concept of communication. He suggested three concepts in development communication more consistent with the new paradigm: self-development, the "communication effects gap" hypothesis, "new technologies" vis-a-vis "social technology." The emphasis on self-development carries with it a concept of development as something groups at the local level do for themselves rather than have a government do for them. Self- development is allegedly more effective, economical, and flexible than centralized programs. This concept of development implies a radically different understanding of communication than the mass media-oriented, top-down models in the dominant paradigm. Interpersonal, bottom-bottom communication is the primary means by which development occurs, and these patterns should be part of "multiway" flows of information. Mass media is seen as "more permissive and supportive" than in Rogers's use of the SMCRE model; it functions to provide technical information in support of local programs and to circulate information about successful self-development accomplishments.

The newer concepts of communication and development make salient the "communication effects gap" hypothesis (Rogers 1976). The hypothesis states that one effect of mass communication is to widen the gap in knowledge between the elites and the marginals. The better educated, who have greater literacy, access to media outlets, and cosmopolitan attitudes are likely to be much greater consumers of communication than those who have the least modern attitudes. Such "gaps" are not inevitable, but the possibility that they might occur sets an agenda for planning and research.

The concerns with diffusion are overlaid in Rogers's new paradigm thinking with a consideration of the "new technologies" of communication. Although these technologies have not yet had significant impact on developing countries, they seem very potent. Some suggest, for example, that microcomputers might enable some nations to skip the stage of large, centralized industry with its attendant rise in urbanization and bureaucratization and go directly from a village economy to decentralized industrialization. Others suggest that the developing countries

39

will gain a technological advantage by installing state-of-the art technology while the more developed countries are struggling with massive capital investment in obsolete machinery. But there is sufficient experience with technological innovation to know that a new technology does not stand on its own merits; rather, it is deeply embedded in social and political structures which can limit its adoption or compromise its potential beneficial effects for a society. Rogers calls attention to the "social technology" which will surround the introduction of the hardware, arguing that this is perhaps the most significant feature.

These concerns are far removed from the linear SMCRE model of "diffusion." They stress the importance of two-way communication for diffusion. Some models build in a "diagnostic stage" for assessing the needs of the masses and for eliciting feedback from them. Rogers (1976) characterized diffusion as a "communication strategy for development," but—reflecting the emphases of the new paradigm—identified two elements quite different from his earlier thinking. First, diffusion occurs in a dialogue with the masses in which they identify their needs. Second, the masses engage in a self-reliant problem-solving activity using local resources and innovations.

COMMUNICATION AS DIALOGUE. In 1978, UNESCO identified the "communication needs" of people in the new paradigm as "open dialogue" between the people and the government. The first way in which such a dialogue was conceptualized was in terms of the "direction" of the flow of messages and diversified content. The "multidirectional" or "multiway" flow of messages prescribes that messages should flow from bottom to top as well as vice versa, and horizontally at every level of hierarchy. Diversification of content refers to the use of communication channels to do more than simply inform and persuade the masses to adopt innovations. Their experiences, thoughts, and motives should find opportunity for expression as well. To implement multidirectional and diversified messages, the UNESCO recommendations specified that "access" to media be made available, even in rural areas.

Dissanayke (1981) noted that various new paradigm statements like the UNESCO declaration imply a shift of meaning in the concept of communication that goes beyond "adding" new directions of message flow and types of content. Instead of a linear one-way model, a process-oriented two-way model like that of Berlo (1960) and Barnlund (1970) is imagined as operating in development programs. The difference is that communication is seen as an interactive process in which the source and the receiver share in the responsibility for what happens.

Singh and Gross (1978) advocated models of two-way communication between policy makers and the public, stressing the importance of feedback in the communication process. There are several loops of feedback and feedforward, allowing the senders of messages—whether in a top-bottom, bottom-top, or horizontal network—to learn how the message is being understood.

Rogers (1976) suggested that the new paradigm leads to an awareness of additional functions of communication. In addition to disseminating information about development programs and persuading people to comply or adopt innovations, communication functions to educate and motivate them for development. Schramm (1983, 14, 15) said that "communication is now seen as a transaction in which both parties are active. . . . It is illuminating to think of communication as a relationship built around the exchange of information. The process of exchange is more likely to resemble a biological than a physical one, to make a difference in both parties, to change the relationship rather than changing one participant."

It was under the new paradigm that the international development community for the first time placed a greater emphasis on interpersonal than mass media channels of communication. Dissanayke (1981) noted that interpersonal channels create a common identity by stressing shared values and experiences of the people, while mass media are best for presenting information. A number of studies, including Beltran (1976) and Bordenave (1976), showed that mass media is most effective in promoting change incrementally, within existing social structures.

However, the existing social structures are often incompatible with dialogue. Silberman (1979) stressed the importance of two-way communication between the authorities and the people. The normal pattern in developing countries is top-down. But if participation in development is to occur, the people must be able to convey information to the policy makers, not only about their preferences and values but also their views on problem solving. This is the difference between dialogue and simple feedback: in dialogue, both parties are engaged and likely to be affected by the interaction.

The emphasis on participation led many development specialists to see that dialogic communication is an inevitable part of development. In this, they have (perhaps inadvertently) agreed with Mao's injunction to "learn from the people," in which he, like Tolstoi, showed a keen appreciation for the accumulated experiences of the people.

There are some important problems in trying to implement the concept of dialogue in development. First, there is an inherent paradox in development (Ploman 1979). To achieve development, there must be a stong central power capable of bringing about changes and a rational allocation of limited economic resources. On the other hand, the construction of a participatory society requires freedom and decentralization as an essential condition to develop the capacity of the society to organize itself. Local autonomy, self-reliance, and socially effective participation are inalienable parts of such freedom. The efforts of a strong central government desiring to promote development may be inimical to the attitudes necessary for popular participation. The best-intentioned government efforts to promote popular participation risk counterproductive effects, and the more intensive the government efforts, the more likely are these unwelcome effects.

Second, the realities of national economics limit the power of local communities and individual citizens. Silberman (1979) noted that modernization has led to economic centralization, which means that citizens have considerably less access to national planning agencies and bureaucracies than businesses and other vested interest groups. Coombs (1980) claimed that educational programs for rural people are more desirable than propaganda strategies for development participation. So long as the poor are economically impotent and politically voiceless, they can hardly be expected to be self-assertive or self-reliant.

Third, a lack of quantity and quality of specific information inhibits popular participation. Narula and Dhawan (1982) noted that development information is complex and may not be available to all of the people, particulary those most removed from modern institutions. Ryan and Kaplun (1980) described the entire communication apparatus for participation as a "closed circuit." Access to the flow of information is generally limited to the elites, and the elites profit from it disproportionately.

Fourth, development programs have not adequately focused on "development motivation" and the growth of a "development psyche." Many development programs concentrate on technical information, as if the reasons for adopting an innovative practice or artifact are self-evident to the masses. Those programs which do address motivation tend to create discontent about a particular condition—for example, the brackish water from tube wells—rather than a general motivation for development. Pareek (1962) claimed that development motivation is a complex combination of achievement motivation (concern for excellence), extension motivation (concern for others), and a lack of dependency motivation (concern for direction from others); he offered a formula for predicting participation in development: $(AM \times EM) - DM$, or achievement motivation multiplied by extension motivation, minus dependency motivation. Muthaya (1981) described development psyche as a forward-looking, self-help and action-oriented bent of mind. In a later chapter, we will argue that motivation for development is even more complex, deriving from patterns of social interactions.

Fifth, status differences pose an obstacle to participation, which the new paradigm has not adequately addressed. Within communities, partisan relationships, caste memberships, resentments stemming from inequitable economic status, and the traditional power structure can preclude the cooperation necessary for popular participation. It is this feature that makes development paradoxical, as Ploman (1979) noted. A vigorous program of restructuring local communities to alleviate some of these problems—including the economic and informational isolation of the marginals—creates a climate of dependency upon the government; but a more tolerant, hands-off approach, which relies on the local groups to take the initiative for development, can be stymied by these factors.

INTERNATIONAL EQUITY

The modernization perspective, in both the dominant paradigm and the new paradigm, attempted to foster development while working within the existing international structures. "Modernity" was seen as a complex set of personal attitudes, technological innovations, and social institutions that originated in the West and now—for any of several reasons—could and should be shared with less fortunate nations.

However, the new paradigm is quietly subversive. It presents a rather fuzzy image of desirably dialogic communication patterns in which the masses are active participants. At least at this level of specificity, the image can be applauded by several types of social libertarians. But the actual occurrence of these patterns poses a major threat to existing political institutions that are otherwise perpetuated by the docile acquiescence of the masses.

The spokespersons for the paradigm we refer to as committed to "international equity" blatantly opposes the existing social structure within many nations and between the third world and the more industrialized nations. In fact, it explicitly blames the international economic order for creating and perpetuating underdevelopment. The spokespersons for this paradigm do not so much disagree with the modernization perspective as find it largely beside the point. Taking a generally Marxist point of view, the spokespersons for this paradigm identify underlying economic relationships and contradictions as the "real" structure, and social realities as illusionary ideologies. Unlike the modernity perspective, the theories described here do more to explain the *cause* of underdevelopment than to guide programs intended to alleviate it. If the problem is the social structure itself, then revolution may be the best response.

44

The Interdependency Model

Nordenstreng and Schiller (1979) argued that the issue of economic development cannot be understood on a nation-by-nation basis. Rather, the network of interrelations among nations must be analyzed.

The interdependency model is a critique of the dominant paradigm's identification of *domestic* factors as the causes of underdevelopment, but it goes beyond being just a critique. The claim is that the *international* sociopolitical system decisively determines the course of development within each nation.

ASYMMETRICAL INTERNATIONAL RELATIONS. The development of individual countries depends largely on economic and political factors outside their national boundaries. For developing nations, the implication of this notion of a world system is that domestic development projects—no matter how well-conceived—may be ineffective, overpowered by the effects of actions taken by other nations. For developed nations, the implication is equally striking: their sense of acting as autonomous agents is erroneous since they, too, are caught up in an interlocking web of multifaceted international relationships. Wallerstein (1979) claimed that the modern world comprises a single capitalist world economy. Nation states are not societies having separate, parallel histories but are parts of the whole reflecting the whole. Some states are at the center of the system and some at the periphery, but all are defined by the relationship among them.

From such a world-systems approach, development and underdevelopment are not independent entities but two facets of the same process and cannot be understood in isolation one from the other. Galtung (1971) argued that these relationships are in fact the more subtle expression of the inequitable patterns of international relations developed during Western colonialism. Economic, military, and information relations all serve as instruments of manipulation in order to maintain the central position of the former colonial powers. This line of reasoning suggests a radical perspective from which to think about international communication.

INFORMATIONAL COLONIALISM. Communication is seen in terms of the patterns of information flow between nations, and is interpreted as a means of perpetuating the existing asymmetrical relations among the "central" and "peripheral" nations. The patterns of such information flow are responsive to the pressures of the marketplace, which is dominated by the developed countries. To the extent that "cultural agendas" for action and collective definitions of self are affected by the content of mass media, they are organized by the international corporations that produce and sell information (Nordenstreng and Varis 1973).

Freire (1971, 144) differentiated "suppression" and "manipulation" as ways in which "dominant elites try to conform the masses to their objectives." Suppression is oppression by total restraint and subjection of the weaker; while manipulation is the use of myths that "explain, justify, and sometimes even glamorize the prevailing conditions of existence" and thus "secure popular support for a social order that is not in the majority's long term real interest" (Schiller 1976, 1).

The view that international communication reinforces existing inequitable relations among nations is frequently identified as the product of a symposium on Mass Communication and International Understanding held in Ljubljana, Yugoslavia, in 1968. Most of the delegates were from nonaligned nations, most of which are also developing nations. The agenda comprised discussions of various efforts to achieve what is now known as a "new world economic order." Impressed by the arguments about the role of communication as seen from the perspective of the interdependency model, the delegates concluded that no fundamental improvement of their economic position was possible without a concomitant (or prior) adjustment of communication policies. They called for the establishment of a "new international information order" (NIIO) as a prerequisite of economic development.

The idea of the NIIO is more an objective than a clear plan to be implemented, but it has provoked a loud and far- ranging debate (Tessier et al. 1985). In recognition of the importance of the issue, the United Nations proclaimed 1983 World Communications Year, and the United States listed efforts toward the NIIO as one of two reasons for its withdrawal from UNESCO in 1985.

More Second Thoughts about Communication

There is a curious relation between the dominant paradigm and the interdependency model. Proponents of the interdependency model explicitly reject the dominant paradigm's assumption of the causes and cures of underdevelopment and reinterpret the function of communication claimed by Lerner and by Schramm. Rather than acting as a means of making individuals modern, communication is seen as a technique of oppression that manipulates the minds of persons in both the developed and developing countries. Ironically, the proponents of the interdependency model share the assumption originally made—but subsequently abandoned—by the dominant paradigm theorists that communication is a monolithic, powerful social instrument. For example, the foremost spokesperson of the NIIO, Masmoudi (1979) alluded to "a veritable invasion of radio broadcasts and television programmes . . . amounting to a violation of national territories and private homes and a veritable form of mental rape"!

What of the rather powerful data that forced the dominant paradigm theorists to revise their assumptions about the nature and impact of communication? Two conclusions are possible.

Perhaps communication seemed complex and relatively ineffective to the dominant paradigm theorists because they were looking at it in the wrong way. To be sure, mass media programs did not powerfully produce the modernizing effect anticipated. But if communication is really an instrument of "manipulation" reflecting the economic inequality among nations rather than a vehicle of information that liberates individuals from the shackles of tradition, then the lack of improvement in the economic conditions of the developing nations is precisely what would be expected. Rather than indicating the ineffectiveness of communication, the failure of the dominant paradigm to guide and explain development can be seen as evidence that communication functions in ways that would not be captured in dominant paradigm evaluation research. When looking for "diffusion," one is not likely to detect ideological "manipulation."

A second possible conclusion is that the proponents of the interdependency model have uncritically adopted the earlier, naive concept of communication as a linear process with effects commensurate with the content of the messages transmitted. This latter conclusion is made more plausible by examining the various measures of information flow used in the NIIO debate. "Bias" is measured not by the content of the news item but by the nationality of the journalist reporting a story as well as by the rates various nations have to pay to use satellite transmission. Alleged effects such as "mental rape" are supported by counts of the proportion of news stories from Western agencies used in the newspapers in third world countries or by vivid anecdotes of unquestionable power but uncertain representativeness. When more straightforward measures are used, the alleged bias and pernicious effects are not found (e.g., Sreberny-Mohammadi 1984).

In our judgment, the criticism of the existing world information order makes important claims and illustrates some disturbing and unintentional effects of communication practices. However, the "debate" serves many agendas other than the most apparent, and has not included a penetrating analysis of communication per se (Tessier et al. 1985).

The most confident conclusion one can draw from this perspective is also the most profound. The NIIO debate itself illustrates the Marxist claim that the functions served by particular communication acts and institutions are not necessarily obvious and not necessarily those intended or understood by those who participate in them. Communication is often portrayed, in general and in specific instances, in ways that are inaccurate. The fact that we *can* communicate in a state of "illusion" about our real motives and against our own best interests has great implications that extend beyond the question of whether in any specific instance we are in fact the victim of manipulation or in a state of illusion.

The Dependency Model

The dependency model can be seen as a more specific aspect of the interdependency model. It makes the radical suggestion that development is more the problem than the solution and offers guidelines to direct actions quite dissimilar from those of the dominant paradigm.

THE DEVELOPMENT OF UNDERDEVELOPMENT. The motivating concern behind the dominant paradigm was the question of how to accomplish development. The interdependency model posed the somewhat different question of why development programs had not worked, and answered with reference to seemingly inexorable inequitable relationships within the world economic system. This perspective frustrates many in the international development community because—short of joining the debate about a new international information order—it gives no guidance about what to do if one is involved in the effort to alleviate poverty and disease in a particular community or raise the gross national product of a given country. The dependency model of development would turn this frustration into guilt. It suggests that development efforts themselves are at fault; they have *created* underdevelopment rather than helped alleviate it.

The actual conditions in any country are a state of affairs subject to various interpretations. It is by no means inevitable that particular conditions should be interpreted as criteria of underdevelopment. Nations which have come to think of themselves as underdeveloped have done so because they have accepted the ideology of the highly industrial, capitalist nations. The penetration of foreign advisors and experts (no matter how "helpful" they intend to be), imported technology, and the influx of information creates an economic and cultural dependency on the developed countries, one aspect of which is the acceptance of the definition of underdevelopment.

The ideology of capitalism does provide code words for practices that perpetuate dependency. Given the technological and personnel inequity between the Western news agencies and those of the developing countries, "the free flow of information"

49

becomes a code word for continued domination by the ex-colonial powers that have previously appropriated all of the competitive advantages. In an economic environment in which transnational corporations and international trade tactics place smaller nations at a pronounced disadvantage, slogans of "open markets" and "free trade" are code words for perpetuation of the existing inequity.

The dependency model does not offer "development" as a solution to the problem of "underdevelopment." Rather, it argues that underdevelopment is an erroneous identification of the problem, and that to accept this concept is already to capitulate to the ideology that makes a solution impossible. The characteristics—poverty, disease, ignorance, infant mortality—of various societies calling for change result from "contradictions" in the modes of production that themselves must be changed. This analysis suggests fundamental reorganizations of the social structure of the country in ways that do not take the industrialized Western nations as ideals to be imitated.

COMMUNICATION AND THE IDEOLOGY OF OPPRESSION. From this perspective, mass media are seen as part of the "ideological state apparatuses" by which the state guarantees the reproduction of society's relations of production. The media saturate all citizens with daily dosages of nationalism, chauvinism, liberalism, moralism, etcetera, in ways that reinforce the social patterns in which dependency occurs.

The domestic use of media is supplemented by international communication, largely originating in the United States, and through contact with personnel from the developed countries in political, military and business activities. Mattleart (1977) spoke of the "ideological aggression" which results when transnational corporations impose their own ideological and economic logic. This occurs not necessarily as a matter of intention but as a natural consequence of foreign intrusion into the political sphere through control over modern technology and education.

Communication technology provides a good example of the dependency created by development efforts. Industrialized, capitalist countries sell sophisticated communication technology to nations they define as underdeveloped. Their overt—and perhaps sincere—purpose is to help them overcome some economic or social problem, or to facilitate their entry as a full partner in the world community. The transnational companies that sell the equipment, however, subsequently control the nation's mass media because they are, not quite accidently, the prime provider of programming for it. This programming either subtly or blatantly promotes values consistent with capitalism and creates demand for particular products. For example, it treats social ills as the fault of some person rather than a result of social institutions or class conflicts and frames the issues it deals with in the unspoken but pervasive perspective of capitalism.

The belief that advanced communication technology is an important component of successful development constitutes an illusionary, ideological myth (Schiller 1976). In reality, there is a two-directional commercial imperative in mass communication. While products and services are sold to the consumers through advertising, the mass media create audiences and these are sold to advertisers and sponsors. What is billed as "the free flow of information" is actually a one-way flow of information for "consumerism" (Nordenstreng and Varis 1974).

Consumerism propagates values which only a minority—urban elites—can actualize, and it thus exacerbates social inequality, increases frustration, and thwarts attempts for social cooperaton (O'Brian 1974; Beltran 1971). Those of the poor who are exposed to mass media see a very attractive lifestyle they have no hope of experiencing. But the economics of the media technology is such as to limit its availablity. The urban and rural masses are excluded from the national communication system just as they are from the market economy, creating an "informational poverty" that combines with economic disadvantage (Pasquali 1975).

Dependency theorists argue that the communication industry perpetuates an ideology that falsely identifies the problem of their countries as "underdevelopment" and exacerbates existing social inequities. Rather than development activities, they recommend educational programs that will enlighten the oppressed people about the vicious nature and stifling effect of dependency on the industrial capitalist countries, and which will mobilize support for a structural change in society. Until these structural transformations take place, mass media serve more to oppress than to emancipate the people.

SOME CRITIQUES OF THE DEPENDENCY MODEL. There are several careful critiques of the dependency model. Dissanayke (1981) and Sarti (1981) noted the complexity and variety of relationships both between nations and within an indigenous culture, and questioned the value of a perspective that reduces all relationships to polarities such as dominaters-dominated, powerful-oppressed, etcetera. In the same vein, Weffort (1971) found the emphasis on the anti-imperialism, anticapitalism theme troublesome because it seemed to ignore contradictions within classes in the oppressed nations. Sarti (1981) objected to the notion of ideology as an "external agent" in the process of production which is imposed on the nation. The dependency theorists tend to blame the imperialist ideology rather than the ruling elites or the apathetic masses. The elites are seen as a communication channel, transmitting the ideology of hegemonic centers of capitalism (the U.S.A.), and the masses are seen as passive recipients of mediated messages without the capacity for any other than the most docile responses.

There are three issues in the critiques of the dependency model. The first involves the adequacy of the model in representing the structure of relationships within the societies of dependent nations. The second raises the question about the function of communication that ostensibly serves the purposes of development. Is it a tool that can be used for perhaps laudable and certainly profitable purposes? Or is it, as Althusser (1971) claims, a part of the "ideological state apparatuses" by which an illusion is perpetrated about the relationships among nations and among classes within nations? The third issue turns on an unstated assumption made by dependency theorists that both masses and elites in developing countries are relatively passive consumers of mass-mediated messages and the logics of meaning and action conveyed by technology and the marketplace. Again the familiar questions come: How powerful is communication? and What criteria should we use in assessing the extent of its impact on individuals and a culture?

IMPLICATIONS FOR COMMUNICATION. Happily, our present purposes do not require that we find answers for these difficult and important questions. The very fact that they are reasonable questions to pose enables us to draw an important conclusion about how communication works. The fact that communication *can* serve some ideology (whether it does in fact serve the particular ideology of capitalist imperialism) and that a "pedagogy of the oppressed" (Friere 1971) can enlighten individuals to the illusions in which they have been enmeshed, implies that the process of communication is imbedded in social structures and meanings that do not necessarily appear in the messages themselves. Giddens (1979) stated very well the conclusion we would draw when he said that social action always occurs in the context of "unacknowledged constraints" and "unanticipated consequences."

POVERTY AND THE BASIC NEEDS MODEL

The basic needs model of development is an outgrowth of a specific aspect of the dependency model combined with the continuing concern of those in the international development community to know what to do to meet pressing human and national problems. Even if underdevelopment is caused by the structure of the international economic relationships, some people see themselves as needing to cope immediately with overpopulation, unemployment, hunger, disease, and malnutrition. If revolution is either undesirable or not practical, what can be done now to meet real human needs?

The Theory of Marginality

Capitalizing on the Marxist attention to social structure and oppression, the "theory of marginality" was offered. Such theorists claim that as much as 40% of the population of some developing nations do not participate in the mainstream social, cultural, economic, and political activities.

A comparable observation was made by Lerner (1958) and accounted for much of the effort behind the use of mass media in the dominant paradigm. The concept of "marginality" itself was first used by Germani, Quijano and Weffort (1973) to describe the situation of people living in sections of cities that did not have basic services. Marginal people are characterized by bad housing, unemployment and underemployment, and insufficient income to afford the goods and services considered minimal for an acceptable standard of living. The marginal population is usually uneducated, does not participate in political processes, and is outside the procedures of production.

In its early form, the attitude underlying the theory of marginality was paternalistic and led to practices of giving resources directly to the needy. Germani, Quijano, and Weffort (1973) claimed that the concept of marginality was grounded in the process of extending human rights according to the principles of equality and liberty as well as increasing consciousness or awareness of violations of these principles. They saw this as the process of increasing modernization. Recent formulations of marginality have suggested deeper sociological factors, which may vary from country to country, including economic and informational dependency on the West or the domination of a society by elites who consume the results of developmental successes.

Marginals do not benefit from the supposed trickle-down of economic improvement. Those in the marginal sector of society are isolated from the economy by their level of poverty such that some direct and focused attempt must be made to reach them. Soedjatmoko (1978, 11) argued that development strategies should have multiple goals, including special-track projects to reach targeted groups. In addition to overall or even per capita growth, development projects should involve bottom-up participation, featuring local self-reliance and decision making. Organizing the poor, in particular, serves three purposes: It creates for them a place in the community social life; it overcomes their economic strategy of mere survival; it breaks the pattern of powerlessness, exploitation, permanent indebtedness, and nearly slavish dependency.

Meeting the Needs of the Poor

The Bariloche Foundation in Argentina developed a world model to show the feasibility of meeting basic needs of all the poor people of the world within stated limits of resource availability and environmental constraints. Many development theorists, those at the Dag Hammarskjöld Foundation, the signatories to the Cocoyac Declaration in 1975, and others, endorsed the concept that development must enhance the welfare of the poor and meet their basic needs. In 1976, the International Labor Organization (ILO) joined this commitment and proposed a specific formulation of the basic needs perspective which they called the Basic Minimum Need (BMN) Model.

As expressed by the ILO, the BMN model focused on four types of needs. Normative needs include minimum levels of health, nutrition, etcetera. Felt needs are those the persons perceive themselves as lacking. Expressed needs or demands are those felt needs which the poor articulate to various agencies. Comparative needs are those things a group may not be aware of "lacking" but that are imputed to them as needs on the basis of comparisons with other groups (ILO 1976, 32). This approach differs from other concepts of development in part because it focuses on the physical quality of life (PQLI) as the index of success rather than simply on economic measures such as per capita income. The PQLI index includes life expectancy, nutrition, infant mortality, literacy, and housing. There is increased emphasis on the importance of equity in the distribution of the resources of society. Implicit in these indicators is the important variable of access to information, with the assumption that information is a primary source for development.

The basic needs model of development originated in the third world, and was presented as a non-Western model. Ironically, it was better received among the developed countries than among the developing nations. For example, former World Bank President Robert McNamara endorsed it in his famous Nairobi speech, and a number of developed countries tied their foreign aid to basic needs projects.

Most third world countries rejected the model. When the developed countries tied aid to basic needs projects, they appeared as if they were more concerned about the poor than the elites in the third world. This was interpreted by some as an attempt to keep the third world countries noncompetitive, largely pastoral societies—though a little better fed, housed, and educated. Further, some argued that the needs of the poor required domestic programs rather than foreign financing.

Regardless of the reason, it is obvious that the implementation of the basic needs model requires massive social change. It blames the existing social structure for isolating the very poor and seeks to restructure the society to bring the poor more into contact with services and benefits.

Communicating with Marginals

Basic services are utilized well only if they become an integral part of self-organization and self-management of the poor persons themselves. This can be accomplished only if there is decentralization and integrated development planning.

Decentralization is important to open the way toward local autonomy and active participation. The local social structure is threatened either by too much centralization, which reserves all decision making for the "top"; or by government efforts directed at individual marginals, which further atomizes the local organization. Integration requires structural reform, including land reform, economic revitalization of designated areas, provision of infrastructures such as roads or public transits, et cetera.

With decentralization and integrated programs, a new pattern of communication among various elements in the society must be achieved to bring the marginals into contact with the economy and with information sources. Soedjatmoko (1976) called for macropolicies for communication, noting that an unprecedented inflow of information into the marginal social groups must be achieved. He suggested that traditional societies must be transformed into a new kind of "informational community."

Ploman (1979) argued that this informational community must include multidirectional flows of information, including both horizontal and two-way vertical patterns.

Such a vision of free and multiple channels of communication is sharply at odds with descriptions of actual communication patterns in developing nations, and with the assumptions in most theories of development of how communication works. The implementation of the basic needs model requires both interpersonal and mass media channels of communication, with the bulk of the emphasis on interpersonal channels.

Even though the basic needs model has not been often implemented, the theory of marginality has focused unprecedented attention on the actual social structures of developing countries. Dominant paradigm theorists had known that the social structures of local communities were an impediment to development, but they believed that mass mediated communication was sufficiently powerful to overcome those obstacles. They found they had underestimated the importance of interpersonal influences compared to mediated messages. The theory of marginality suggests another, large group not likely to be reached at all by mass mediated messages. This reasoning suggests two conclusions about how communication works.

First, it shows the importance of the utilization, not merely the existence, of communication channels. The fact that persons live in the same village or town does not necessarily mean they speak to each other, and the fact that a message is broadcast does not necessarily mean people hear it, or, if hearing it, listen to it. Whether there are communication channels or networks between any two parts of a society must be an empirical question, not the subject for assumptions.

Second, it shows the necessity of interpersonal channels of communication. In terms of top-down communication, mediated messages are of doubtful efficacy unless complemented by interpersonal channels. In most societies, bottom-bottom and bottom-top communications depend on interpersonal channels. One of the pressing needs of development communication seems to be finding a way to make bottom-bottom and bottom-top networks form and work effectively.

THE COMMUNICATION PERSPECTIVE

As paradigms of development have evolved through debate and experience, their concepts of communication have been continually revised. There is a clear direction in these revisions; they have consistently shown communication to be more vitally involved in development and a more subtle, complex, and complicated process than had been imagined.

In our judgment, these revisions are fully warranted but insufficiently radical. They are piecemeal, rearguard attempts to patch up a fundamentally flawed notion of communication. The revisions retain the assumptions that communication is a subset of human actions or situations and that the task of a definition is to differentiate a category of events/objects that comprise communication from those that do not.

The propensity to differentiate communication from not-communication follows one of Aristotle's "laws of identity" and brings into the present his fondness for categorizing things. In contemporary thought, the Aristotelian heritage is expressed in the assumption that one communicates by speaking, reading, or using sign language, but not by sleeping, eating, or running. More recently, Shannon and Weaver's (1949) immensely useful mathematical model of communication depended on a differentiation of "information" and "redundancy" in messages, a move which reinforced the notion that some, but not all, of human behavior is communicative. For present purposes, at least, this strategy for defining communication orients development strategists and practitioners into unproductive lines of thought and action.

The problem with this strategy lies at its edges rather than at its core. There is little difficulty in identifying a particular instance of social interaction as communication. The problem arises in specifying what human actions are *not* communication. It has turned out to be impossible to identify a set of "criterial attributes" to differentiate between communication and that which is not communication. Any form of social action can be shown to be communication. Running (away from a crime or toward a long-lost friend) is clearly a form of communication;

so is sleeping through a class or having dinner (with the new person at the office). Etcetera.

The liberating move is to define communication not as a category of acts but as a perspective from which to look at any given act. Everything one does or does not do can be looked at as having "message value." One can communicate powerfully by burning a bus, as irate commuters did recently in Calcutta; or by not being in one's office when the residents of Jhangirpuri want to register a complaint.

From the communication perspective, human actions are seen—whatever else they may mean—as the process by which persons collectively maintain and create "social reality." Human beings simultaneously live in a symbolic universe (social reality) and are engaged in sequences of interactions with their environment and with other people. They actively strive to create coherent "stories," drawing from the resources of their social reality and from the practices in which they are engaged with others. They tell themselves stories that explain and guide their performance in practices, and they enact stories that exemplify and "test" their resources.

This orientation can be given graphic form. Figure 3.3 shows how persons draw from their resources to guide them in interactive practices, and interpret their practices back into their resources.

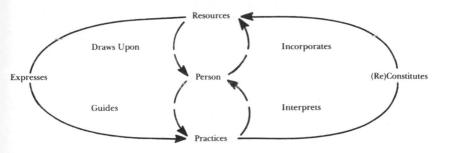

Figure 3.3 The communication perspective.

Implications of the Communication Perspective

All knowing comes from some perspective. Researchers or planners tend to see only what their terministic screens allow them to name, and to do what their paradigmatic vocabulary predisposes. The communication perspective facilitates interpretative and critical analysis.

The purpose of interpretive research is to show how particular acts express and [re]construct the social realities of the actors. This function requires and enables the researcher to become a part of the interactions studied.

> [T]he social scientist . . . redescrib[es] an act or experience by setting it into progressively larger contexts of purpose and intelligibility, he reveals *what* the agents are doing by seeing what they are up to and how and why they would be up to that. . . . The result of this sort of analysis is thus a kind of enlightenment in which the meanings of actions, both of one's own as well as of others, are made transparent. . . . [*a*]n interpretive social science thereby increases the *possibility of communication* between those who come into contact with the accounts of such a science and those whom it studies . . . Moreover, in all of this it is not just being able to communicate with others, but also thereby opening oneself up to their influence, which is significant. . . . To make available a new form of language is to make available a new form of life. (Fay 1975, 79–81)

In the best of cases, interpretive research facilitates improved communication among the subjects of the research.

The purpose of critical research is to articulate what the participants themselves do not know or cannot articulate about their own resources and practices. Critical social scientists "recognize that a great many of the actions people perform are caused by social conditions over which they have no control, and that a great deal of what people do to one another is not the result of conscious knowledge and choice" (Fay 1975, 94). Giddens (1979) observed that social action always occurs in the context of "unacknowledged constraints and unintended consequents."

An analysis of development from the communication perspective enables otherwise obscured or problematic aspects of development to be seen clearly, even to appear obvious.

From this perspective, many social actions that otherwise would not be defined as instances of communication are shown to be powerful means of creating and managing social reality. The Indian government engaged in at least three types of social acts in its development effort. It engaged in direct action such as building roads to make transportation easier between previously isolated villages and larger urban areas. It enacted legislation designed to break up "exploitative linkages" by which the elites profited from the discomfort of the poor. Finally, it engaged in what it perceived as "development communication," a process of message transmission through several channels from the government to the masses.

How should this development communication be evaluated? In terms of the extent to which people were exposed to those message? comprehended them? believed them? acted on the basis of having heard them? Surely, but in a more fundamental way as well.

The communication perspective leads us to ask how any form of social behavior "expresses" and "[re]constitutes" the social reality of the actors. In what way did development communication and the other forms of action taken by the government express the social reality of the planners? of the masses? To what extent did development communication constitute the social reality of the masses? of the planners? of the change agents who delivered the messages?

Consider the public works and legislation. The Indian government clearly did not think of these as "communication." But looked at from the communication perspective, both powerfully expressed and constructed the social realities of the masses and of the government officials themselves. The fact that *only* "development communication" was seen by the government as communication is itself a revealing clue about the social realities of the government's development strategists.

The communication perspective also leads to an analysis of the "constraints"—acknowledged or unacknowledged—that social realities impose on participants in communication.

As Geertz (1975) said, persons become human not by learning culture "in general" but by learning a particular culture. This process facilitates movement within the institutions and folkways of that culture, but can also be seen as imposing limits. If one group of infants learn to be Indian, they simultaneously learn not to be British or Russian or Chinese, and vice versa. This learning imposes constraints, because as adults these persons will find it impossible to learn another culture in the same way. Their first learning shapes them in ways not under discretionary control.

The phenomenon is perhaps best understood as "enmeshment" in a particular system. A person is enmeshed in a system to the extent that its boundaries comprise the horizons of the person's vision. To the extent that dominant paradigm theorists could think of no other pathway of development than the Western model of industrialization, they were deeply enmeshed in that system. The lack of empathy among traditional people that so concerned Lerner can be seen as the result of deep enmeshment with the social reality. Lerner's advocacy of mass media campaigns was an attempt to reduce the extent of their enmeshment in their "native" social realities.

Those who are comfortably enmeshed within a particular social reality see *its* limits as the limits of the *world*, not as a more or less arbitrary boundary between what they know and what they do not. One of the purposes of doing an analysis from the communication perspective is to discover and articulate the limits of various social realities, and to show how these limits sometimes channel people into unwanted patterns of interaction.

On Taking a Communication Perspective

The communication perspective takes its substance from the questions it puts to any given human act, not by delimiting itself to a specified subset of human acts as its disciplinary province.

Rightly understood, any message reveals the whole social reality from which it originates. The corollary of that statement, however, is a bit unnerving. To understand any message rightly requires knowing the whole social reality from which it originates. The interpretive aspect of analysis from the communication perspective is an attempt to describe at least the most relevant parts of the social realities of the participants in an interaction. But it is not sufficient simply to restate what the actors know. The process of communication is an excellent means for coordinating interpersonal action, but it is a very poor means of expressing individual mentation or for achieving mutual understandings. For a complete analysis, the researcher must discover what the actors themselves do not know about themselves and their interaction.

Such complete information is not normally—if ever—available, and thus researchers seek the best available data. Usually this includes a record of the actions performed in sequence by the agents involved; a description of social realities of each agent, inferred from all available texts, including interviews when possible; and a description of how the agents' social realities are affected by the acts they perform.

FOUR

Indian Models of Development

AT THIS WRITING, India is in its fourth decade of planned development.

At Independence, the economy was in "a vicious state of self-perpetuating stagnation" (Ministry of Information and Broadcasting 1971, 4). The legacy of foreign domination was a major part of the problem. Colonial rule was quite explicitly exercised in a manner to strengthen the British Empire, not to serve the interests of individual Indians or to develop a domestic economy. The British built ports and railways that proudly ran "on time." However, this infrastructure was geared not toward the needs of an autonomous economy but to facilitate imports of industrial goods and exports of raw materials. This exploitation destroyed indigenous industries. Small farmers could not compete with large estates, and the British monopolized materials needed for domestic production of manufactured goods. Many rural farmers lost their land to moneylenders, and others were unable to earn enough to maintain more than a subsistence living. Since most consumer goods were imported, the economy provided relatively little employment opportunities or return on investments.

Education provided upward mobiity for some individuals but did not lead to strong social institutions. Education was not available for most Indians, and the curriculum for the privileged few was defined by the needs of the Empire. Lord Macaulay expressed the goal of education under British rule: to create "a class of persons, Indian in blood and colour, but English in taste, in opinions, in morals, and in intellect" who would "be interpreters between us and the millions whom we govern." (*India since Independence* 1971). So conceived, the educational institutions were not likely to produce far-reaching programs of social change.

On top of all this, the partition of Pakistan led to an influx of an estimated 8.5 million refugees, placing even more demands on the government's resources.

Widespread poverty and economic disorder posed a major challenge. In the official *India since Independence*, Prime Minister Jawaharlal Nehru described the new government as engaged in a "tryst with destiny." He said, "The service of India means the service of the millions who suffer. It means the ending of poverty and ignorance and disease and inequality of opportunity. The ambition of the greatest man of our generation has been to wipe every tear from every eye. That may be beyond us, but as long as there are tears and suffering, so long our work will not be over." Development in India has seen experiment, change, and dogged determination. (See Figure 4.1.) During the first development decade the stress was on national development through social growth. The models of community development and the Panchyat Raj system were in essence participatory communication and basic needs models, although not labeled as such. At this time, most of the international development community was adopting the dominant paradigm. In the second development decade, Indian planners switched over to the dominant paradigm, stressing individual modernization and national industrialization. In the 1970s and 1980s, the development models stressed participatory communication and basic needs—comparable to the new paradigm and the Basic Minimum Need model.

THE GANDHIAN METAMODEL

India experimented with the Gandhian plan of rural reconstruction during the three years between Independence and the first formal development plan. The Gandhian concept of "Sar-

CODING KEY FOR FIGURE 4.1
INDIAN DEVELOPMENT DECADES

Gandhian Metamodel	GMM
Etawah Project	EP
Nilokheri Experiment	NE
Community Development	CD
Panchayat Raj	PR
Cooperatives	COOP
New Paradigm	NP
Dominant Paradigm	DP
Agriculture Extension Model	AEM
Administrative Decentralization	AD
Basic Minimum Need Model	BMN
Extension Model	EM
Diffusion Model	DIM
Integrated Development Model	IDM
Multidisciplinary Approach at Local Level	MAL
Operationally Integrated Strategy	OIS
Block Plans	BP

(Broken lines denote a period in which a subsequently revived model was dormant.)

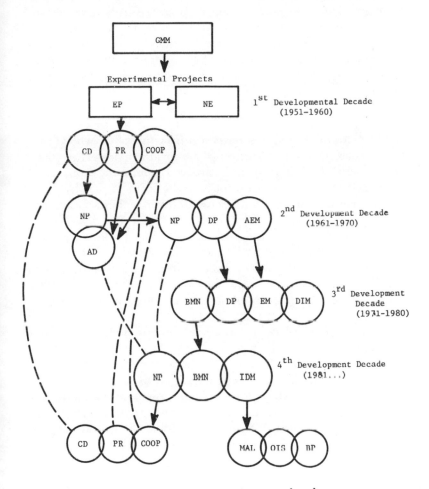

Figure 4.1. Indian development decades.

67

vodoya" describes a democratic socialistic pattern of economics and institutions suited to the conditions, realities, and needs of Indian society. The plan sought to preserve Indian values and ways of life rather than replace them with Western models. It stressed rural reconstruction rather than heavy, urban industrialization, and rather than specific economic indicators it established as its goal a just social and political order devoid of exploitation.

The Strategy of Rural Reconstruction

The Gandhian plan was based on his concept of "villageism." In practice, this was an attempt to produce powerful village communities by initiating participatory communication, developing self-reliant village republics in the form of panchyats (local governing councils), enforcing reform of land ownership, and encouraging the development of rural industries. The village was seen as the unit of social planning. It should be self-reliant and provide the basic necessities of food, shelter, clothing, education and justice. Village industries would provide employment. The natural and necessary cooperation among villagers in everyday matters of social, economic, and political life would produce popular participation.

In plans for rural reconstruction, development was thought of in terms of human beings. The first objective was to improve the quality of life by providing the basic minimum needs. Next, the programs attempted to reorder society by structural changes such as removing exploitative linkages, caste impediments and social and economic inequalities. As Savita (1970, 13) noted, the goal was a social order in which the good of the community was given priority over private profit. The Gandhian model suggested vigorous attempts to mend, and if need be replace, outlived social, economic and political institutions. In their place, the society would strive for justice, freedom, and equality for all citizens.

Three aspects of the traditional social structure were identified as contributing to the problems of the people. First, the feudal system institutionalized social roles in which people were "linked" by the exploitation of one by the other. For example, landlords instigated economic dependency by demanding money from the very poor for various reasons. When these people could not pay, they often went to the village moneylenders who charged usurious interest rates. The short-term solution to the fiscal problem thus created a more serious long-term problem. Too poor to pay subsequent demand levied by both the landlords and the moneylenders, they often wound up in bonded labor to both. The second problem of the traditional social structure was that the rigid caste system institutionalized "marginals" who were then completely isolated from the economy. Finally, the traditional attitude toward family and children resulted in a population that—literally—swallowed any increase in material resources.

Although the British left peaceably, they left behind little to facilitate development. Fiscal and technological resources were limited. Mass media channels were insufficient to connect the people to the government and to each other. Political instability was caused by religious and ethnic diversity and by the "Princely States" within the country, the heads of which resisted "rural reconstruction" as a threat to their hereditary privileges. The government viewed them as uninterested in the welfare of their subjects, exploiting them so that they could enjoy a luxurious lifestyle vastly different from those whose labors produced it. Outside the urban areas, where "armchair clerks and civil servants" were educated by the British, there was almost universal illiteracy.

Further, there was no adequate administrative structure through which the commitment to development could be implemented. Mayer and Merriott (1958) gave a most discouraging assessment. Development was thought of abstractly. Some departments had grand plans for development with no implementation strategies or with no conception that the plans should be fitted to people's needs or to varying conditions. Attempts to implement development were ineffective. They were not energetic, in part because the development agents were aloof from the people and lacked understanding of the people's require-

ments and viewpoints. Higher-level administrators lacked practical experience and delegated unrealistic amounts of work to
their subordinates. The people were far from sure that they
should trust the government agents or that the development
plans were in their best interests. Lower-level field workers were
not listened to by their supervisors, nor did they take effective
initiative to make themselves heard. As a result, they lacked
moral commitment to or involvement in village-level work.

Mayer and Merriott found a great deal of deception and self-
deception among those entrusted with the development effort.
Field workers and supervisors told themselves that they were
making great progress in development. In fact, they were working very unsystematically and ineffectively.

Massline Communication

Consistent with his emphasis on nonviolent techniques of persuasion and conversion, Gandhi, and his plan, stressed interpersonal channels and oral communication. These channels describe a top-down "advisory" role for the government but also
include bottom-up channels from the people to the government
and bottom-bottom channels among the people themselves.

Savita (1970, 11–12) suggested that Gandhi wanted mass participation in development through mass consensus. In this physical, economic, and spiritual resources of all sections of the society in the service of the comon good. This concept carries with
it a radical decentralization of power. Gandhi envisioned a government that would build from below and govern as little as
possible. In this way he hoped to avoid corruption and abuse of
power.

Gandhi did not describe the "interpersonal infrastructure"
that would permit this massline communication pattern to function, but he was quite clear about its purposes. It would raise the
consciousness of the people against exploitation, injustice, and
poverty; encourage conscious efforts for socioeconomic equality
and social change; and enable people to articulate their needs
for development.

These purposes are most specifically focused on the Untouchables and suppressed classes in order to bring them into the mainstream of society. Two communication efforts were recommended. First, the government should initiate special- track interpersonal communication programs in the form of mass meetings, group persuasions and personal examples by great public leaders and voluntary workers. Second, special programs of interpersonal communication as well as print media should be initiated to get the Untouchables and other lower castes accepted by the elites and other high-caste groups as part of society.

Criticisms of the Gandhian Metamodel

Narayan (1960, 55) summarized (and attempted to rebut) three criticisms lodged against the Gandhian plan. First, critics claimed that a decentralized economy would create an economic vacuum that would elicit a great deal of materialistic values. Second, industrial backwardness would upset the world equilibrium and engender imperialistic activities toward India. Third, decentralization was not feasible because the village panchyats were not competent to organize the village economic, social, and political life in the face of local factions, petty rivalaries, and civic irresponsibility.

In addition, the model can be critiqued for ignoring two factors that have subsequently been shown important. The only aspect of traditional attitudes and practices addressed by the plan was that related to caste; there are other aspects of the social and intellectual tradition that impede development. In addition, Gandhi's emphasis was almost exclusively on rural communities; his plan did not address the unique situation of the urban poor.

EXPERIMENTAL PROJECTS

Gandhi provided the metamodel of Indian development. It was never implemented as such, but its various parts were the basis of much of the subsequent development experience in India. Three experimental projects based more or less explicitly on the Gandhian model were conducted as pilots for future development efforts.

The Etawah Project

A pilot project was conducted in Etawah, Uttar Pradesh, with Albert Mayer as consultant. It was a village development project combining aspects of the American "agricultural extension" program with the pattern of Indian administration.

OBJECTIVES AND METHODS. The project's objective was to enable villages to achieve economic efficiency, improved quality of life, and active participation by the people. Economic programs focused on increasing productivity and income through improved agricultural procedures and by developing local industries suited to local needs. The concern for physical quality of life led to programs in health, sanitation, nutrition and related community facilities.

A key factor was people's participation in development. The role of the people was envisioned as both articulating their needs for socioeconomic facilities and meeting these needs through their own efforts. The people's participation in these ways was thought necessary so development would be continuing and self-propagating. Without this type of involvement, improvements would disappear when the involvement of the central government ceased. A major part of the Etawah project was directed toward changing the people's attitudes from indifference and distrust to interest and trust in development efforts.

Three criteria were used to evaluate various development activities; they should: build confidence and know-how; be based on realistic planning; and address felt needs.

Confidence could be built by implementing some programs that would show quick results, thus encouraging an attitude of receptivity and alertness among the villagers. This required administrators to use policies of setting priorities and following time schedules, selecting and enacting only those practices that were well-suited to the situation, that the people were likely to adopt, and for which the necessary supplies were available. Know-how could be inculcated by demonstrating better ways of doing practical tasks. The planners thought that villagers would be willing to accept innovations if they were shown better ways of doing old tasks.

The project stressed realistic planning, based on the characteristics of the local situation. The problem was to avoid constructing a general plan for development and imposing it in a rubber-stamp manner. To counter this tendency, planners were urged to observe each group of villages to insure the proper sequence and timing of development projects.

Participation was elicited by focusing on the felt needs of the people. Three objectives were set: development awareness, self-development, and self-reliance. The people were encouraged to be alert and to "awaken" from their fatalistic philosophy and identify their needs. It was thought that people would become more aware of development needs if the government priority for programs reflected the felt needs of the people and directly affected their welfare. This close linking of felt needs and beneficial effects was also thought to lead to a role in which the people would actively seek new and better methods and ideas for development, naturally taking the initiative in development. To initiate self-development and self-reliance, the administrators would have to synchronize their programs with the people's readiness to participate.

Participation could be encouraged by structured activities. The Etawah project attempted to develop leadership within the villages and to stimulate planning and cooperation among villages.

Mayer and Merriott's (1958) evaluation found in the administration of development projects some major problems. First, there was a conspicuous absence of intellectual honesty and critical self-appraisal. Second, frequent movements of personnel resulted in nonspecialization. The notion was that a person trained in administration can administer anything; this frustrated technical personnel who often lost confidence in their administrators because they knew little or nothing about the specific projects to which they were assigned. Third, the vertical communication patterns were too weak. Administrators did not welcome—in fact, were perceived as discouraging—advice or opinion from lower ranking or field workers. Fourth, the relationships among administrative personnel did not express an "inner democratization." Although the government as a whole was pledged to a democratic socialism, the relationships among administrative personnel did not reflect sufficient interpersonal warmth, restraint on arbitrary decisions, and wide consultations. Mayer stressed the importance of "democratic initiative" at all levels, expressed as devotion, enthusiasm, and strong sense of status and recognition regardless of rank. Fifth, the personnel had not sufficiently reflected the change in the character of government from a police or revenue collecting agency to a welfare government. The incompatibility between the new system and the patterns of interpersonal relationships and administrative procedures among the remnant of the older "law-and-order" government impeded many development efforts. Sixth, there was a lack of specific targets and of evaluation by objectives. Mayer called for studies of public opinion during the course of development projects to assess the masses' responses to development.

COMMUNICATION AND PARTICIPATION. The Etawah project suggested three roles of communication: mobilization, education, and persuasion. Mobilization consisted of providing opportunities for coordinated activites within and among villages, and between the masses and the government. With the emphasis on assessing the effects of programs, and carefully planning the sequence of programs, communication from the masses to the government was as important as the flow of messages from the government to the people. Education implied making people aware of and motivated for development. Persuasion consisted of strategies of inducing people to become self-reliant, to undertake self-development, and to produce local development leadership.

Most communication channels were interpersonal, consisting of the multipurpose village-level workers, the extension agents, program specialists (both technical and general), and the village panchyat. These persons held public meetings, demonstrations, discussion groups, and Kisan Melas (farmers' fairs). They performed Route Marches in which a party of development organizers walked from village to village, formed song clubs, produced folk dances, and reinterpreted old legends to reflect development morals. "Wall newspapers" provided a vehicle for local expression, development news from other places, and two-way communication between the masses and the government.

The Nilokheri Experiment

Between 1948 and 1951, the swamp land between Karnal and Pipli in East Punjab was reclaimed and a new township—Nilokheri—built to serve 100 villages in the area. The inhabitants were the displaced persons from Pakistan. The township was both a means for rehabilitating refugees and of conducting an experiment based on Dey's (1962) concept of development.

The basic idea was for self-reliant agroindustrial townships to serve as the nerve centers of rural development services, providing technically trained manpower, creating a traffic of goods and ideas, and being sustained through agricultural supplies and the products of cottage industries. The economic base of villages and towns would be strenthened by a strong reciprocity.

In addition to economic motives, as Dey (1962) and Jain (1967) noted, the objective of the project was to engender a spirit of fellow feeling and a higher level of employment and income for the people. Vocational training centers and cooperative enterprises were set up to provide employment in the town as well as in the surrounding areas.

In 1950, the Narielwala committee report strongly recommended adoption of this model of agroindustrial centers as the pattern of development for rural areas. However, this recommendation was not accepted. The government felt that "the time was not ripe" and that rural development following the model of villageism was the higher priority (Dey 1962).

The "Grow More Food" Campaign

In addition to these two experiments, the Krishnamachari committee report, which evaluated the Grow More Food campaign, was another formative factor in Indian development. The Grow More Food campaign was a national program that set as the highest priority the production of more food—by assisting farmers to increase their production. The evaluation of the program found that the village farmers had their own priorities, such as village schools, health services, road, and water. The national goal of growing more food to feed the urban population simply did not inspire those who cultivated the fields. This finding by the committee confirmed an earlier report by the Fiscal Commission on Agricultural Development in 1951 that had suggested the chief problem was psychological.

According to the Krishnamachari committee, farmers could be motivated to apply the improved techniques necessary for increased food production if they were helped to find solutions to the problems about which they were most disturbed. Once they were assured that the government was interested in helping them, they would respond to government help to produce a greater food surplus.

There were also administrative problems with the campaign. Each department approached the villagers through its own hierarchy of status, and the lowest officer in the organization was the person in actual contact with the villages. This contact agent was usually incapable of providing guidance because he was inadequately trained. This, plus other ways the program of technical assistance was administered, tended to assure that the campaign benefited only the larger landholders.

The committee recommended an integrated administrative framework for making a concerted effort in development and urged the establishment of a national extension service.

First Five-Year Plan: 1951–1956

On the basis of the Gandhian metamodel, the experimental projects, and the Grow More Food experience, the government committed itself to a series of five-year plans for development. The first plan focused on community development.

Community development programs were visualized as physical and social reconstruction of the community by developing relationships between groups and individuals that enabled them to create and maintain facilities and agencies for the common welfare. The basic philosophy of these programs was "power to the people," and they envisioned the masses becoming engaged in a continuing process of finding solutions to their own problems, drawing on the government as a resource but not becoming dependent on government to solve their problems for them. The people themselves were identified as a primary resource to be developed, comprising vast unutilized energy lying dormant in the countryside that should be harnassed for constructive work.

This concept of "constructive work" and the people as an "untapped reservoir of energy" derives from a progressive ideology quite unlike the fatalistic traditions that characterized the rural areas. Community development thus became an exercise in transporting an ideology that would make possible a new role between government bureaucracy and the masses. This was an explicit attempt to create a new and vital culture, to bring about economic and cultural transformation of the village structure, and to produce political advancement, improved standards of living, and new patterns of employment.

Under the Block Development program, the entire country was divided into "blocks," of 100 villages each, comprising about 250 square miles and about 60,000 to 70,000 residents. Each block had a development bureaucracy that was supposed to provide resources on which the increasingly self-reliant villagers could draw. The model was the American extension program as adapted to India in the Etawah project. This model had three major features. First, research and extension were linked with agriculture in universities and institutes. Second, a class of progressive farmers would be created who would gladly accept the findings of scientific agricultural research and put new technological innovations into practice. Third, an extension agent, guided and trained by experts would be sent to the villages to demonstrate new techniques, first to the local leaders and then to the villagers.

Communication was conceptualized as a linear, top-down process with feedback from the people. The first five-year plan document included a chapter referring to "plan publicity," which should use all communicative channels: interpersonal, mass media (radio, film, print), and traditional media (song and drama). Feedback from the people was seen as important not in setting development goals but in successfully adapting the government's

77

message to the local requirements and achieving popular support. In 1951, Prime Minister Nehru told the planning commission:

> The peasant in the field may not understand all the details of the plans, but he can tell us that what we are doing is right for him. You must keep in mind the urges of the people and if you fail in this respect, you fail to secure popular support and the whole purpose of planning is vitiated and would collapse. Further, the principles of development planning should be adapted to each country's background and conditions, to the urges and genius of the people (*India since Independence*).

The role of communication was thought of in three ways. The first function was to develop communication channels, including decentralization of planning, and to incorporate "upward" information and feedback from the people to the planners. The planning document stressed that "the plan has to be carried into every home in the language and symbols of the people and expressed in terms of their common needs and problems." The technological infrastructure for a nationwide mass comunication system was developed, and informational programming was prepared for it. Interpersonal channels were developed through intensive training programs for extension agents. Local leadership was recruited in an attempt to create indigeneous enthusiasm for innovations among the people.

The second role of communication was to disseminate development information through extension education methods. Ad hoc committees, project advisory committees, and official and unofficial agencies were assigned the task of publicizing the plan and dispelling the people's suspicions about development and the development functionaries.

The third role was to let the development functionaries recognize the value of the knowledge, wisdom and experience of the common man. As the document read,

> [I]f anything goes wrong anywhere, or obstacles are encountered, it would be helpful, if information is imparted candidly and people are acquainted with the steps being

taken to set things right. It is an error to belittle the capacity of the common man to find out and accept what is good for improvement.

Evaluations of the success of community development programs indicated that the forms of communication in practice differed from those envisioned by the planners. They were most successful in establishing channels by which information could be disseminated from the top down. They were least successful in implementing aspects of the plan that involved educating and motivating the people for development.

SECOND FIVE-YEAR PLAN: 1956–1961

The emphasis in this plan was on rural participation and democratic decentralization. The planners continued to perceive communication in terms of "plan publicity" through multiple channels. The extension agencies, technical departments and administration were seen as supports for the Panchyat Raj, not as the primary structures for development.

Information on agricultural innovations was disseminated by extension agents, through the mass media, and by means of demonstrations supported by the technical staff. Interpersonal channels were used to inform and motivate farmers to adopt innovations. For the first time, the press was identified as a component of plan publicity.

As part of democratic decentralization, a number of things were done that the planners did not think of as part of their communication. For example, in order to circumvent traditional social structures, they formed intervillage cooperative organizations and imposed the Panchyat Raj system of government by local village councils. The panchyat served as spokepersons for the villagers and as an intermediary between the villagers and the government. Further, village election systems were initiated; since every villager had a vote, this gave even the lower castes the opportunity to excercise political power.

The purpose of the Panchyat Raj was not fully achieved. The elites were disproportionally involved in the process, intensifying what has been called a "communication gap" or "development benefit gap" between the "haves" and the "have-nots" in the villages. The actual communication pattern that developed is diagrammed in Figure 4.2. As part of economic policy, two land reforms were enacted. The Land Ceiling Act fixed an upper limit on the amount of cultivated land that could be owned

Villagers ↔ Panchyat ↔ Government

↗ ↘ ↙

Selected Elites   Selected Elites

Figure 4.2. Communication patterns of the panchyat.

by any individual. The lands confiscated under this act were to be distributed to the landless farmers. The second act abolished the Zamindari system, the feudal landlord arrangement. The Zamindar owned the village lands and reaped the benefits, although the work was done by others who received meager benefits. The Abolition Act specified that only the person who works the land can own it, within the limits set by the Land Ceiling Act. The planners did not see these reforms as part of their communication.

Interpersonal channels of communication were used to explain this legislation and these structural changes to the people. Contact change agents attempted to convince the masses that they had been exploited in the past, and that the government was taking steps to prevent continued exploitation. These messages, but not the legislation and restructuring of the village leadership, were thought of as communication.

THIRD FIVE-YEAR PLAN: 1961–1966

The concept of "plan publicity" continued. The planning document stated, "As part of the program for strengthening the public co-operation and participation, it is proposed to intensify the existing publicity arrangements for bringing home the implications of rapid development and carrying the message of the plan to the masses throughout the country." Both mass media and interpersonal channels were used to publicize the plan, but there was a special emphasis on radio.

In 1966, Farm and Home Programs were introduced. These were broadcast by radio stations located near areas of intensive farm activity. The programs discussed solutions to particular farm problems, applied nutrition, and other aspects of rural life for both men and women. The objective was to give rural people a vision of the future and enable them to become active participants in development projects.

Other radio programs specifically targeted factories, schools, colleges, homes, and offices. By becoming a forum expressing a variety of views, radio gained some measure of credibility, making people feel that their perspectives were being heard. In 1969, the Yuv-Vani programs atempted to reach young people, who had become very restive. Prime Minister Indira Gandhi supported the use of radio to influence young people in order to give them the feeling that they are not the problem but rather participants in the country's decisions (Desai 1977).

All India Radio broadcast programs in the dialects of each region specially devised for various social groups, such as women, slum dwellers, youth. These programs carried information about family planning, drinking, dowries, etcetera, giving the people the impression that they were a part of a broad social movement.

Starting in 1959, television was introduced in a UNESCO-aided project. In 1961, Delhi school television projects were started for science education, and in 1965, the Krishi-Darshan, a special agriculture program, was introduced for the Delhi audience.

The press made little contribution to development publicity (Desai 1977; Raghvan 1976; Mehta and Narula 1968). Their emphasis was on politics and politicians, with little effort to educate the masses or serve the unique needs of a developing nation.

DISCONTENT AND EVALUATIONS

During this period, there was widespread discontent with various aspects of the development programs. This led to some penetrating evaluations.

Sahai Committee Report on Public Participation, 1964

Starting with the assumption that development programs were not effective, the Sahai committee sought to explain the reason why. They found that the masses had little understanding of development as a whole, viewing it simply as something government was doing for their own reasons and to their own benefit. The masses accepted innovations that met their felt needs or gave immediate results but did not see themselves as "partners" with the government in a common endeavor of national reconstruction. As a result, they did not give much respect to public property or money. The rural elites exploited the less educated and less powerful members of their communities rather than helping them, and the poor continued to be preoccupied with survival rather than development. This characterization of the masses is, of course, a description of "passive participation."

Development administrators were found to have little knowledge of development programs or plans. The plans themselves were made without local participation and were unsuccessful in achieving widespread public cooperation.

The committee concluded that something must be done to develop a "new social faith" among the people that would enable them to subordinate their personal interests to the common good.

Report of the Study Team on Plan Publicity Impact, 1964

The Team concluded that "plan publicity" had failed. The report claimed that "the needs of the society we have and the society we are seeking to establish are neither efficiently nor adequately being served by the existing publicity programs . . . The impact . . . on the public has been tenuous, vague and confused. In an unplanned attempt to achieve too much with too few resources, plan publicity has failed to touch any section of the society in a forceful manner." Four reasons were cited for the failure. First, the publicity personnel were viewed by the public as propaganda agents; as a result, public cooperation and favorable public opinion—"the principle force and sanction behind planning"—remained a wish, and the objective of getting "the administration and the people to feel and act together" remained unachieved. Second, plan publicity was based on inadequate research and implemented with insufficient coordination. Third, the mass communication media were judged poorly adapted to the needs of plan publicity; the media institutions showed little interest, familiarity, or sympathy with development objectives. The report noted that low literacy, pervasive poor education, and the lack of adequate technology posed additional problems. Fourth, inadequate funds were allocated for plan publicity.

Ensminger Evaluation of Community Development Programs and Panchyat Raj, 1972

Douglas Ensminger noted that "community development" had been introduced in the first development decade as a dynamic force that would revolutionize village India. It was expected to lead people into new and improved ways of living. In the second decade, the political leaders and development planners and administrators became disillusioned about community development, and these programs were blamed for India's failure to solve the problem of insufficient food. Ensminger argued that both the administration and the people were responsible for the disillusionment which led to a de-emphasis on community development, particularly the Panchyat Raj system.

The administrative bureaucracy was ill-equipped to let people-oriented village programs emerge. They did not share the philosophy—difficult at best—of organizing the people to assume initiative, and they did not take comfortably to the role of "change agent" to villagers who traditionally were expected to obey them. They often did not treat the people as intelligent and capable of acting effectively. Most of the personnel had been officers in an administration oriented toward "law and order." They felt comfortable setting targets and pressing the people to meet them, but such use of authority does not lead to self-reliance and active participation. Worse, targeted programs displaced more general goals of social education, which were less immediately and less conspicuously effective but nonetheless essential for achieving self-perpetuating development.

Administrators relied heavily on village-level workers, perhaps too heavily. The village-level workers were placed into multiple, conflicting roles. On the one hand, they were to awaken, motivate, and educate the people; but on the other, they were pressured to meet specific development targets. To fill the latter role, they often engaged in practices such as collecting savings, monitoring agricultural supplies, encouraging people to repay loans, etcetera. These practices made them known as functionaries of the administration, not as educators, and thwarted them from fulfilling their other role.

The administrative bureaucracy and political leaders did not like working with the panchyats; they accused the panchyats of serving partisan interests in the villages and of maintaining caste structures. Ensminger argued that the real problem was that the panchyat were becoming a source of power in the villages, and reflected deeply embedded caste and factional structures in Indian life. In essence, the administrators did not like dealing with some of the realities of village life. On the other hand, the villagers were not ready for self-reliant development. The idea that government would be a "helper" in a partnership for a transcendent national goal was a new and seldom comprehended concept.

Other Evaluations

Norman Nicholson (1973) concluded that the Panchyat Raj had not been a successful means of generating community efforts to solve local problems. Rather, it intensified political conflicts within the village and thus inhibited cooperative action. In part, this occurred because the local elites made disproportionate use of the cooperatives and the panchyats, which increased the gap between the elites and the poor.

A second problem noted by Nicholson was the extent to which community development programs, designed to foster local self-reliance and initiative, ironically led to dependency. He noted that when public enthusiasm and community action was stimulated by massive infusions of government resources, this proved inimical to the community development philosophy of a "mix" of self-help and administrative control. Further, the national plan of a controlled and coordinated economy was incompatible with the rhetoric of local initiative in the community development program. Finally, he observed, the way the government contributions to communities were administered often created a conflict between the needs and interests of individuals and the needs and interests of the community. Given such conflicts, most people act selfishly.

Akhter Khan (1978) claimed to find four "crucial imperfections" in community development programs. First, they were more effective as welfare programs than in eliciting productive activities by the masses. Second, they did not succeed in forming harmonious communities; the poor remained as they were, apathetic and skeptical. Third, by relying on their own agents and by collaborating with established leaders, the community development programs enhanced the traditional elitist and paternalistic bias, inhibiting the growth of local initiative. Fourth, experts were unwilling to work with the untrained community development functionaries.

Iqbal Narain (1970) found the Panchyat Raj ineffective from two perspectives. From the vantage of the people, the panchyat was seen as the extension of the government into the village. This made any efforts by the panchyat seem part of the government-guided development, not an aspect of local initiative. To the extent that the panchyat was active, it increased the dependency of the people on the government. From the vantage of the administration, the panchyat was the lowest, least-educated, and least-effective tier in the organizational structure, not a vital or important part of planning or implementation.

ANNUAL PLANS: 1966–1969

Between 1966 and 1969, three annual plans were formulated, taking into consideration the poor state of the economy and lack of resources available for development. The planning commission was constituted with all new members, and they were expected to reorganize the planning effort to make it more effective (Minhas 1974, 7). This was not an easy task, since there was a serious recession, high inflation, a growing trade deficit, an increasing national debt, and an extreme shortfall in agricultural production.

FOURTH FIVE-YEAR PLAN: 1969–1974

The fourth five-year plan showed a greater sophistication about the use of communication media for plan publicity. "Information imbalance" was identified as the problem. The plan stated,

> In the spread of information facilities, the imbalance in favour of urban concentration and prosperous areas continues. There is need for a deliberate attempt to inform the people in the rural areas and particularly those in backward regions about the development activities so that the benefits of these development programs are more widespread.

Calling for an integrated approach, it recommended selecting optimal media mixes and avoiding duplication and waste.

During this and the subsequent fifth plan, extensive campaigns were undertaken for development programs in family planning, health, nutrition, adult education and agriculture. In addition to using virtually every available public channel, this was the first time that the interpersonal channels of communication among friends, family, and opinion leaders were identified and utilized. These channels came to the attention of the planners for two reasons. First, they realized that the extension agencies and government development personnel were not sufficiently effective. Second, family planning is such an intimate aspect of life that more personal channels were appropriate.

The emphasis shifted from informing and educating the

86

masses to motivating them to adopt development practices. For the first time, "motivators"—groups of voluntary workers—were used as a communication channel (in the family planning program). Both the motivators and the adopters were given incentives in cash and commodities such as transitor radios for adopting the practices or technology advocated by the development programs. Other communication channels included group discussions, mass meetings, mobile demonstrations, family planning camps for mass sterilization operations, and interpersonal contact on a house-to-house basis. Rural opinion leaders were taken to motivational camps to increase their effectiveness (Mulay and Narula 1972).

The plan publicity procedures were so energetic during this plan, that by the time it ended some were concerned about an "information glut" (Vittal 1981). The public was being satiated with development publicity. During the fifth plan period, many research studies attempted to assess the extent of satiation.

FIFTH FIVE-YEAR PLAN: 1974–1978

This plan had to cope with disastrous rates of inflation. In 1975, Prime Minister Indira Gandhi imposed a "state of emergency" and announced a "20-point development strategy," designed to achieve short-term objectives that would bring direct relief to the masses.

Films were used to create audience's awareness of the 20-point programs. Short films were shown in the cinema houses and were screened in mobile vans in the villages.

SIXTH DRAFT FIVE-YEAR PLAN: 1978–1980

The new government, elected in 1977, replaced the concept of periodic five-year plans with rolling five-year plans reformulated each year. The election of this government was seen as an expression of popular discontent with development; the victorious party campaigned on the slogan "Remove Poverty." The plans for this period are referred to as the "Sixth Draft" because they were never implemented; the new government was voted out of power before the five-year plan was completed. Analysts believe that the short tenure of the new government was due to widespread belief that the new government could not achieve their goals to "Remove Poverty" even as well as Mrs. Gandhi's Congress [I] Party, which had been defeated in 1977. The Congress [I] Party was soon returned to power.

During this period, explicit attention was given to communication, but primarily to identify ways in which it was problematic. This emphasis led to a flurry of sophisticated but depressing lists of all the things wrong with development communication. For instance, the report of the Asian Regional Seminar in Rural Communication (1977) faulted the media, the message, the audience, and the communicators. The audience was seen as having insufficient access to the media, a lack of aspirations, poor motivation, inability to formulate and articulate their needs and grievances, vested interests opposed to change and progress, and problems stemming from illiteracy. The media were seen as ineffective channels for communication, in part because there were too few of them and the existing ones were too little utilized, too costly, and without sufficient intermedia coordination. Messages were evaluated as not addressed to the neediest people, not in the language or idiom of the audience, incompatible with the values and traditions of the people, contradictory, and repetitive. Communicators were described as having low credibility and little knowledge of rural areas, and of being poorly motivated, unskilled, too few, and inattentive to feedback from the masses.

Evaluation research showed that some communication practices were particularly ineffective. Mulay and Narula (1972) found that motivators were doing more harm than good, particularly in family planning programs. Their persuasive techniques sometimes amounted to coercion and exploitation. After initial success, the scheme of giving incentives in cash or kind for adoption was not effective. For several reasons, the people were often disappointed with the incentives. In some cases, they felt that the contact agents had given them only part of what had been promised, keeping the rest for themselves. One program specialist was banned from a village. He had distributed battery-operated transitor radios as an incentive for males who had a sterilization operation. When the batteries lost their power and the radios no longer worked, the men wanted the operation reversed, and felt that they had been irresponsibly exploited when told that it was irreversible.

A disappointing pattern was found in special development programs that included massive information campaigns. Their initial effect on awareness, knowledge, and adoptions was quite high, but this was quickly reversed when many abandoned the innovations. Continuing the campaigns was relatively ineffective; those who had not adopted the innovation early were not likely to do so later. Some development planners attributed this pattern to the "satiation effect" produced by an "information glut", particularly in family planning and agriculture. Field studies, however, showed that the people were not satiated with information per se but with poorly devised mesages. What they needed, the people themselves insisted, was more relevant and timely information.

This period marked the first time that the development problems of the residents of rurban (urban slum) areas were differentiated from those of urban and rural people. New urban development resettlement colonies were planned to provide basic minimum needs to the slum dwellers. However, these plans gave no attention to communication infrastructure. In fact, rurban development programs were sometimes administered using the infrastructure of urban and sometimes of rural programs, even though they differed from both and required a special structure (Malhan and Narula 1969).

The assigned role of communication in this period was to inform, educate, and motivate people. Based on research and experience, three distinctive emphases predominated. First, the disappointing results of target-oriented persuasion in development campaigns led to an emphasis on promoting general pro-development attitudes. Second, the notion of a "satiation effect" led to a concern with the content of messages. Planners envisioned communication strategies with more variation that would sustain the interest of the people. Third, specified groups were identified as not being reached by development communication. Although there was an "information glut" in the rural areas, there was also an "information blockage" for the rural "have-nots" and for residents of rurban areas. Strategies were developed to enable communication media to reach these groups.

SIXTH FIVE-YEAR PLAN: 1980–1985

This plan was based on an unprecedented amount of research evidence about the nature and importance of communication in development. Previous plans referred to communication only as the "publicity" of government plans. Even within the limits of this concept, no overall conceptualization or policy coordinated the use of various media. The sixth plan was the first to articulate a program of "development communication."

This plan responds to the broadly based dissatisfaction with the results of previous development programs, some of which was based on a series of research studies conducted in 1975 to assess the need and status of development communication and communication policies in India. The most significant of these studies was by Dubey (1976), who argued that development programs fail to produce desired results if they are not supported by adequate and effective development communication programs. The prerequisites of such programs include adequate communication networks, conducive communication situations, and appropriate communication policies.

Dubey argued that existing communication networks, media, and practices enlarged the gaps between the small, mostly urban group of modernizing elites and the large, mostly rural, tradition-bound masses. The rural elites had been counted on as intermediaries between these groups, but they served as poor "bridges," because they had vested interests in continuing several aspects of the traditional way of life. Further, communication patterns within the development bureaucracy were poorly defined and communication between the planners and the research personnel completely ineffective.

The problem with the existing communication situation is difficult to specify because there is no scientific knowledge of what the situation is. The mass media are heavily relied upon for development communication, but their operation is not well understood by the masses. The media are urban based and elite biased, and they speak primarily to males. Beyond these disquieting facts, not much is known.

Again, the problem with communication policies is not so much that they are wrong as that they do not exist. Dubey suggested that the time-bound, unsystematic series of development plans that included communication only as publicity did not constitute an effective program for development.

In 1979, there was a series of conferences and research reports appraising development communication. In February, the Indian Institute of Mass Communication and the International Institute of Communication (London) organized a conference on Rural Development and Communication Policies. The participants noted several problems in development communication. In top-down patterns, development messages do not reach those for whom they are meant; and when they reach the targeted audience, they are often not utilized. In horizontal patterns, there is an inordinate amount of information loss between development agencies.

These problems were traced to three weaknesses: qualitative shortcomings in the content of information and messages; quantitative shortcomings in the access to media and lack of information about the origin, transmission, and perception of the messages; imbalances in communication between the urban and rural areas, between regions, and between groups based on social class, power, sex, and age.

The conference proposed a series of recommendations designed to rectify the imbalances in the flow of information. One of its suggestions was the establishment of "communication resource centers" for every village or group of villages to provide access to media and to serve as a clearinghouse for information. Another recommendation urged "densification" of communication. Still another proposed that planning be based on research about the audience profiles.

In March 1979, an international conference on Communication and Development was held in Delhi. The major question was whether the disappointing implementation of development plans was due to communication failures or due to other problems in Indian society. In light of three decades of development experience, this question was asked: Is it possible to leave communication to the existing structures or is it necessary to have a public policy regarding development communication?

The question was answered at a third conference of communication specialists and administrators from south Asia in 1980. The agenda was the MacBride Commission Report, and the conference reached a consensus that each country should evolve a national communication policy. India endorsed this view, in part based on the analysis of the deficiencies of various channels of communication as instruments of development.

In the milieu of these studies and conferences, which gave unprecedented attention to and sophisticated analyses of communication, the writers of the sixth five-year plan assigned communication the role of involving people from all walks of life in development. This was to be accomplished by greater use of media to motivate people rather than to disseminate information, by a greater emphasis on interpersonal communication, and by monitoring and evaluating programs in a continuous manner so as to provide feedback adequate to improve program performance.

The plan and related policy decisions impose new criteria at many parts of the communication process. The major thrust of the plan is based on the concept that the people must be brought into a more active participation with development efforts. The plan acknowledges major obstacles but calls for the creation of a more dynamic and more equitable society by an all-out war on poverty, by mobilizing all the latent energies of the people, and through a blend of political will, professional skills, and people's action. The plan is synchronized with a new model of Indian development aimed at the same goal with which the nation began: a just social and economic order based on the principles of socialism, secularism, and self-reliance.

Summary

MODEL	CONCEPTUAL PERSPECTIVE	GOVERNMENT EFFORTS	EVALUATION
Gandhi Metamodel	:Accepted as a conceptual model :Village development through participatory communication :Development of human beings by improving physical quality of life (basic minimum needs), Quality of life (by giving structural changes) :Agriculture and rural industrialization	:Implement metamodel by devcom model through 5 yr national development plans	:Preexperimental situation was that development plans were not need-oriented :People were not ready to accept development :People lacked faith in government development plans; they were not benefiting from them :Development administration was not oriented to development tasks. They lacked understanding of people's needs and viewpoints. They were indifferent to the people :Lack of communication within development administration :Development procedure was unsystematic

MODEL	CONCEPTUAL PERSPECTIVE	GOVERNMENT EFFORTS	EVALUATION
Etawah Project (1948–52)	:Effective development depends on coordination of active village participation; development administration, and strong village leadership	:Implement the three dimensions through 5 year plans	
Nilokheri Experiment (1950)	:Agroindustrial economy for rural development	:Not adopted due to various constraints	
1st Plan	:Creating development awareness among people (by informing, educating, motivating) and acceptance of need for development :Development of communication channels—mass media (radio, print, film) interpersonal, and traditional :Effective public participation	:Extension education approach :Development of extension agencies :For interpersonal communication links :Development of radio technology :Promotion of traditional media :People's contribution in cash, labor, and kind	

Plan	Item	Status	Remarks
2nd Plan	:Panchayat Raj for decentralized rural administration	:Implemented	:Only radio was effective; press neglected the rural scene
	:Land tenure reforms for structural changes	:Implemented	
	:Structured leadership by training rural leaders	:Implemented	
	:Structured citizen participation	:Committed	
	:Reorientation of development administration to dev tasks	:Implemented	
	:Devcom programs for women	:Committed, partially implemented	
3rd Plan	:Adequate information to understand development message	:1 & 2 implemented by extension agents, media channels (radio, TV, film, print)	:People adopted the development programs
	:Attitude and behavior change		:Program specialists effective in assessing felt needs. People did not give feedback either through media or interpersonal channels
	:Active people participation in program implementation	:Implemented through above channels	
	:Government assessment of people's felt needs, feedback by interpersonal and media channels	:Implemented	

MODEL	CONCEPTUAL PERSPECTIVE	GOVERNMENT EFFORTS	EVALUATION
	:Development of TV for devcom	:Implemented	:Serious development information imbalance. Urban and progressive rural regions have more information than backward urban, rural regions
	:Development of traditional media for social communication	:Committed	
	:Organized media feedback programs	:Implemented	
4th Plan	:Attitude and behavior change	:Intensive and extensive campaigns using media mix, interpersonal channels	:Devcom personnel did not have adequate devcom skills
	:Motivating people for adoption		:Lack of coordination between communication agencies and development agencies
	:Interpersonal (personal) channels of family, friends, opinion leaders used as devcom links		:Interpersonal (impersonal) channels ineffective

5th Plan	:Development awareness, information, and adoption :Adopting different devcom model for rurban communities :Removing structural constraints by legislation/education	:Intensive and extensive media mix campaigns	:Devcommunity felt there was information glut, but there was information imbalance, blockage by have nots :Satiation effect in development :Development ineffective due to communication problems: *People* :Inadequate access to mass media, interpersonal (impersonal) channels :Lack aspiration/motivation :Inability to articulate needs, grievances :Rural elites oppose change, progress *Media* :Inadequate existing media :Inadequate use of existing media :Lack of coordination among different media
	:Formulation of national media and communication policy	:Official efforts	

MODEL	CONCEPTUAL PERSPECTIVE	GOVERNMENT EFFORTS	EVALUATION
			Messages :Not oriented to weaker sections :Overloaded with information :Inconsistent, untimely, poor treatment *Development Bureaucracy* :Credibility gap :Low awareness of rural problems :Inadequate communication tools :Inadequate attention to feedback :Inadequate facilities to train rural communicators
6th Plan (current)	:Development support of media in communication :Communication action programs for meaningful participation of people	:Experimental stage :Experimental stage	

The Social Reality of Development Planners

DEVELOPMENT IS AN EXERCISE in practical economics, the discharge of political commitments, an act of national altruism, and more. But if examined from the communication perspective, development is a sequence of acts, each of which expresses and [re]constructs the "social reality" of the actors. This chapter describes same aspects of the social reality of those involved in planning the development programs for India.

The commitments of the new government required the planners to excercise imagination. At Independence, the only available models of comprehensive national economic planning required governments to exercise totalitarian authority. These models were of little value, however, since the new government was committed to democratic socialism. The Indian government strove for "democratic planning," a system "where progress is achieved through the willing sacrifice and co-operation of the people; where the Plan is thrown open to public debate and discussion and adjusted in that light to secure the widest public participation" (*India since Independence* 1971, 22).

The goal of the planners was to initiate "active participation" in development by persons from all sections of society. To this end, the people in the villages have been encouraged to express their needs, propose solutions, evaluate the success of particular programs, etcetera. In practice, however, planning has been done primarily by state or national government officials who are part of the urban elite, although strenuous attempts have been made to include contributions from people in various levels of government.

The people we refer to as "planners" are government officials appointed to the Planning Commission, other political leaders in the national and state government, and technical experts consulted by the commission. Our description of the social reality of these planners is based on a content analysis of public documents, which include the published plans themselves, evaluation reports, and statements in various forums. Our procedure, contextual analysis, seeks to determine what specific acts were taken to mean, in what context, and in what sequence.

Democratic Socialism: To Achieve a Just Social and Economic Order

The planners have an explicit commitment to the larger goals of the national government and take a perspective that encompasses the broad range of government activities. They see India as suffering from problems resulting from the colonial occupation by a foreign power. The British experience, they feel, produced a self-perpetuating poverty, a social system full of exploitation and inequity, and an economic infrastructure poorly designed to enable India to function well as an economic entity. In addition, they feel that the international political and economic environment impedes their independence and prosperity. Within these unfavorable contexts, however, they are committed to achieve "democratic socialism."

Articles 38 and 39 in India's Constitution clarify the meaning of "democratic socialism," and were cited when the government created the Planning Commission in March 1950. Article 38 says:

> The State shall strive to promote the welfare of the people by securing and protecting, as efficiently as it may, a social order in which justice, social, economic and political, shall inform all the institutions of national life.

Article 39 makes this commitment:

The State shall, in particular, direct its policy towards securing—[a] that the citizens, men and women equally, have the right to an adequate means of livelihood; [b] that the ownership and control of the material resources of the community are so distributed as best to subserve the common good; [c] that the operation of the economic system does not result in the concentration of wealth and means of production to the common detriment.

Prime Minister Nehru described the "socialist pattern" to which the government was committed in this way:

Our ideal is that every man, woman and child in India should have equal opportunities, and that big disparities should go. It is not an easy objective, because it means improving the human being by training, education and in a hundred other ways. Socialism depends on how we organize our own system of sentiments and thinking, how we act towards our neighbour and how we develop our capacity to work together. Socialism implies co-operation and removal of barriers. The main thing to remember is that we have to bring about the changes by peaceful and co-operative methods (*India since Independence* 1971, 15).

The effort to achieve democratic socialism necessarily took two aspects: policies directed at the national economy as a whole and policies directed at community development. Problems of the national economy revolved around such issues as balance of payments, international trade agreements, monetary and fiscal policies, gross national product, and building an infrastructure for industrialization. Problems of local development included the harmful effects of caste structures, social patterns in which some individuals exploit others or engage in economic practices profitable to them personally but harmful to the welfare of the community, resistance of villagers to helpful innovations, and obstacles preventing particular segments of the society from participating fully in the economic improvements in their communities.

Planners have always seen these two areas as interrelated but have had different notions at various times about which should be given priority in their plans. This decision is important, because the national economy and community development imply different kinds of government activities.

During the first development decade, the planners seemed to think of national economic issues and local development problems as interdependent, each a prerequisite of the other, and gave them roughly equal priority. The improvement of individuals' lifestyles was thought impossible unless there was a strong national economy, and a strong national economy depended on the adoption of modern innovations by the people. For example, villagers had to improve their agricultural production so the balance of payments would not be adversely affected by having to import large quantities of food, and the national economy had to hold the inflation rate down so any gains made in earning power would not be lost by the rise in prices.

During the second five-year plan, the Mahalnobis economic model for development was proposed. This model stressed industrialization. The public sector would take a major role by providing financing through a liberal bank credit policy and by building the infrastructure necessary to create a strong industrial base.

The Mahalnobis model received strong support for several reasons, including the prime minister's desire to make India a strong industrial power, improving its position in the international marketplace. The plan appeared feasible based on the Soviet experience which indicated that the construction of heavy industries is the means of assuring national autonomy and influence. In addition, economists in India and elsewhere at this time were claiming that a lack of industrialization was the cause of unemployment and low standards of living. They felt that a large increase in the production of capital goods at an initial stage would lead naturally to an even greater increase in the rate of production of consumption goods, and with this an increase in employment opportunities. A political expedient was the close link with the Soviet Union and their willingness to provide foreign aid for this type of development.

In terms of the tension between the economic model and the needs of local development, the Mahalnobis model is clear: the priority is the larger scope of national economic issues. Successful accomplishment of these objectives will, in the long run at least, facilitate development of the masses. Benefits for the masses, and the basis for community development, will "trickle down" through the society.

In the third decade, the planners' perception of the relationship between national economics and community development changed again. The fifth five-year plan (1974–1978) was formulated at a time when the economy was facing serious pressures from inflation. It had become apparent to the planners that the efforts toward long-range planning targets were not bringing immediate relief to the masses. It was during the years covered by this plan, as described in Chapter 3, that the government declared a state of emergency and Prime Minister Indira Gandhi announced the "20-point development strategy," which focused on short-term development programs to bring clear and quick effects for the people.

DEMOCRATIC PLANNING

Democratic planning was attempted by involving the people as well as various levels of government personnel. The procedure of community development was based on "extension" projects in the United States and the United Kingdom. The first five-year plan summarized the strategy: "Community development is the method and rural extension service is the agency through which the Five-Year Plan seeks to initiate a process of transformation of the social and economic life of the villages."

The concept of democratic planning contains some inherent tensions, particularly for "experts" and "professionals." If they are really wiser and more knowledgeable than others involved in the planning, then they face a dilemma. If they let others, less qualified than they, make the decisions, they permit poor planning; but if they insist on their own preeminence, they have taken an elitist position and betrayed the concept of democratic planning. This tension runs through much of the social reality of the planners and produces unanticipated patterns in their logic of meaning and action.

103

THE CONCEPT OF SELF AS A PROFESSIONAL

The planners see themselves as designing a government program that will result in "democratic decentralization." As the designers of a program, they were active, relying on their expertise, willing to use the resources of the government to reach into virtually every village in India, and deliberately attempting to change traditional social structures and ways of thinking.

This strong, centralized activism by professional planners was not commensurate with their stipulated goal of democratic decentralization. For democratic decentralization to work, the initiative of the planners had to be matched by that of the people. The tensions between expertise and democratic decentralization are well illustrated by the experience of the Block Development program discussed in chapter 4 in connection with the first (1951–1956) and second (1956–1961) five-year plans.

The planners were not unaware of the tension. Even their activities which intruded most on the local level—that is, the most powerfully centralized moves—were intended to involve the people in active participation and further eventual decentralization. For example, advisory committees of local people— later known as Block Development Committees—were set up to assist the Block Development Officers and other extension officers; individuals or communities receiving aid for development activities from the central government were required to contribute in cash, kind, or labor; and the Panchyat Raj system was instituted to provide a mechanism for local initiative and a channel for bottom-up communication.

Communication patterns were designed to make villagers aware of and motivated for development. The restructuring of traditional village social structure by the formation of panchayats and cooperatives was seen as a means of providing local leadership for development and a channel for bottom-top communication.

The self-concept of professional Indian planners thus contained conflicting elements: They were at once expert administrators and democratic participants in a larger process in which their own initiative and efforts had to be matched by those of other development agents. The tensions between these elements are not terribly difficult to reconcile within a coherent social reality if it were not for the fact that communication requires coordination—patterned sequences of action with others—as well as coherence. The content of their concept of self made the planners very vulnerable to the actions of other development agents. The ensuing history made it difficult for them to maintain either component of their professional self-concept. We describe below how the interactions with other agents exacerbated the tensions between these contradictory notions and how they, in a resourceful but fateful manner, handled those tensions.

PERCEPTION OF THE MASSES

The planners simultaneously hold two fundamentally discrepant concepts of the masses, each related to an aspect of their professional self-concept.

When they think of themselves as expert planners, they see the masses "realistically," as poorly educated, with a very limited perspective on development, and making unrealistic demands and suggestions for development. Some of the specific features of this perception of the masses have changed during the process of development. At Independence, the planners perceived the masses as fatalistic and thus complacent, uninterested in change; they were ignorant of the possibility and means of improving their lives and enmeshed in exploitative linkages that precluded them from improving their economic or social conditions. As a result of legislation, direct government actions, and development communication, planners now perceive the masses as no longer fatalistic but as discontented with existing conditions and desirous of change; they are largely aware of the possiblity of improvements and freed from exploitative linkages and are vocal in expressing their discontents. However, the demands they make are not always realistic, and the suggestions they make for development programs are often unfeasible and uninformed.

When they think of themselves as part of a society characterized by "democratic socialism," engaged in a process of "democratic planning" that leads to "democratic decentralization," the planners have a "romantic" concept of the masses influenced by the rhetoric of Gandhi. In this context, the masses are seen as one of the great resources of the nation, a reservoir of scarcely tapped energy and the repository of great wisdom; their active, egalitarian participation in the process of development is essential for success.

This perception is not only in marked contrast to the "realistic" description of the masses, it is also at odds with the description based on current research evaluating development programs. This research shows the masses to be discontent, demanding, unwilling to participate actively in development programs that are in their own best interest, and unable to take a larger perspective of development as a national commitment.

The romantic concept of the masses has two aspects, one political, the other pragmatic. Political goals often are served by "convenient fictions" that become self-fulfilling prophecies. The romantic concept of the masses is a vital component of the national commitment to democratic socialism. To the extent that it is an inaccurate portrait of the masses, it sets the agenda for increased effort by the planners. Their social reality as planners is such that if shown incontrovertible evidence that the masses do not possess the laudable qualities envisioned for them in this romantic notion, the planners do not say, "We were wrong!" and abandon democratic socialism. Rather, they take such demonstrations as evidence that their professional skills as planners and their access to the resources of the government should be used with doubled energy to convert the *is* to the *should be*. In fact, the planners are not deluded about the characteristics of the masses but use the romantic concept as motivation for their work; it is in one sense an idealized vision of the national goals as announced by Nehru and expressed in the Constitution.

The romantic concept as the ideal is buttressed by pragmatic considerations as well. The peculiar nature of development requires the planners to take the world view of the masses into account. If they were planning a national energy survey, for example, they could safely inventory the deposits of raw materials as relatively fixed and passive, fairly objectively establish refinery capacities, and make plans that only involved the activities of government agents: surveyors, miners, processors, distributors, and others. But development involves changing the nature of individuals and social structures, getting those individuals and communities to act themselves. As a result, development planning must take into account the "interaction" between the government agents and the masses.

Development planners have long been aware of the fact that the people are unwilling to adopt innovations not related to their own felt needs. As a result, from a purely pragmatic standpoint, the masses must be brought into the development planning process at least to the extent that they express clearly to the planners what they feel their needs to be, and whether they see particular development programs relevant to those needs. The fact that the masses are often unaware of what they need, or mistakenly perceive the relation between a given program and a felt need, is for these purposes irrelevant. Their response to development programs is mediated by their perceptions, and thus their symbolic world must be taken into consideration.

PERCEPTION OF CHANGE AGENTS

Change agents are perceived as the essential means of implementing development plans. They are the communicative channels to convey messages both from the planners to the masses and from the masses to the planners. They are the extension of the government into the communities themselves, and of the communities into the government. This "human chain" of the panchyat and opinion leader through the village level worker, the block development officer, the program head, and so on up to the highest level of government is intended to close the old gaps between the more knowledgeable and the less, between urban and rural, and between the elites and the poor. The change agents are the crucial links in this chain. They are the persons on the spot who are sufficiently knowledgeable about the local scene to adapt development programs to the specific needs and conditions of particular localities.

The planners, however, blame change agents for most of the

problems in implementing development plans; primarily they accuse the change agents of limited knowledge and perspective, unable to see the "larger picture." According to the planners, the change agents are often unaware of the limited resources available for particular development projects and unaware of the demands of other factors such as inflation and the balance of payments.

THE NOTION OF HOW DEVELOPMENT WORKS

The planners have a definite notion of how the various groups should interact in order to bring about development. As shown in Figure 5.1, their implicit model of how development agents interact is democratic. They envision all agents as actively participating in a fully circular process. In this process, their own role is that of providing expertise that guides the action of others.

This model, of course, includes the tensions among mutually exclusive concepts described above. According to this model, the interaction among development agents goes like this:

1. Administrative change agents are informed of the situation in particular communities by feedback coming from evaluation research, from the reports of contact change agents, and from messages from the opinion leaders and masses themselves. On the basis of their information, they perceive the need for a particular project, for example, bringing tap water to the masses. Such tap water projects have two components: They pipe good river water to the community, avoiding the brackish surface water from tube wells; they lay a network of pipes that brings the water into or near homes, so that the people do not have to travel long distances to get water.

2. Administrative change agents inform the planners about the need for a tap water project. The planners design a program for securing tap water and present it to the administrators for implementation. Administrators then engage in a two-step process:

3. Administrators bring the problem to the attention of the contact agents, opinion leaders, and masses. In the villages, this is done primarily through interpersonal contacts.

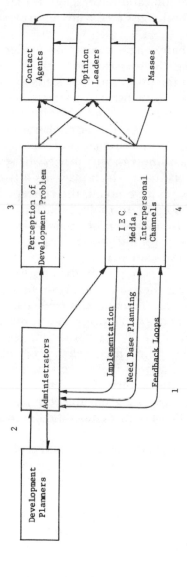

Figure 5.1. Planners' concept of how development works.

4. Administrators design and implement an IEC (information, education, communication) campaign for tap water. In this campaign, they use both mass media and interpersonal channels of communication.

5. The contact change agents, opinion leaders, and masses communicate among themselves and with the administrative change agents about the program. This leads to a goal-directed, self-correcting process in which tap water is made available to the masses, and a greater amount of information about the masses' needs is obtained by the administrators. Linkage #5 becomes the same as #1 in a circular process.

The apparent smoothness of this process belies the complex social reality of the planners, which prevents it from running in just this manner. As we have noted, the concept of democratic planning itself incorporates unresolved tensions. These tensions are "managed" by the inclusion of "time"—by seeing various aspects of democratic planning as occurring at different times in an unfolding, temporal sequence.

In the early stages of development, the masses are not thought capable of identifying their own needs or of making realistic practical suggestions for meeting those needs. In these early stages, linkages #1 and #5 (Figure 5.1) are of minimal value; development programs really start with linkage #2, in which planners—due to their expertise—select programs and convey them to the others. Later in the process of development, the masses will have acquired sufficient awareness, information, and motivation to become a valuable partner with planners in a democratic process. At this point, democratic decentralization will occur.

The first phase of this process involves the planners' concept of self as expert, efficacious government officials and the planners' perception of the masses as unlearned, fatalistic, and in social structures inimical to development. The second phase of the process involves the planners' concept of self and of the masses as equal participants in the democratic, decentralized programs designed to achieve the national objective of democratic socialism.

This anticipated sequence has not been realized, and the particular pattern of outcomes frustrates the planners. The first phase has been conducted successfully. They perceive the masses as having replaced ignorance of alternatives with a great deal of development awareness and information, as having replaced complacent fatalism with a profound discontent about existing conditions and a desire for change, and as having restructured social patterns at least to the extent that all might share in the benefits of development. But they have not become actively involved in the development programs. Their participation takes the form of expressions of discontent—through verbal channels or as part of violent demonstrations—in which they make strident demands that the government provide them specific redress or remedies for what they feel is wrong. These demands are often unfulfillable because of the limited resources of the government, and the suggestions the people make for solutions to the problems are often unworkable. For various reasons, including the limitations of the change agents as means of communication and education, the people have not become active participants in democratic planning, and development has remained centralized.

The Centralization of Development

The planners envisioned a sequence leading to decentralization, in which there would be a "withering away" of the bureaucracy, or at least a change in the pattern of action so that the people themselves would take the initiative for identifying development needs, devising solutions for those needs, and implementing remedial programs. It has not worked this way for a variety of reasons, one of which is the planners unwillingness to relinquish their position.

Three factors make it unlikely that the centralization of the development effort will diminish. First, the necessity to coordinate community development efforts with national and international policies apparently necessitate a strong central planning group. One of the criticisms of Gandhi's "villageism" was that it gave the appearance of a weak state unable to defend itself against the economic or military incursions of other nations. The government has found that the weather, the fact and threat of war, the fluctuations of international economic conditions, etcetera, are related to the lifestyles and prospects of people in the villages, and that community development both affects and is affected by these issues. However, the panchyat and other local development officials are not often informed about these matters, and are unable to see their local needs in the context of larger issues. Precisely because the planners are committed to the goals of the government as a whole, they must remain a centralized body capable of coordinating various aspects of the nations' programs.

Second, any bureaucratic structure develops a great inertia and tends to perpetuate itself. The very activities required for the first part of the evolving sequence of development set in motion administrative procedures and institutions that tend to resist the "withering away" of the centralized authority. The Programme Evaluation Report of the first five-year plan was sensitive to this and warned that an emphasis on organizational compliance and official responsibility is "turning the State induced popular movement of rural regeneration into an official program of tasks in which people are asked to participate." Compounding the universal problems of bureaucracies, British colonial rule left an unhelpful model of the purpose of goverment and the behavior of its officials. Many of the personnel of the development projects came from the ranks of officials of British India, in which government was seen as a ruling entity entrusted with maintaining order and punishing offenders. This legacy was particularly disabling for an effort to induce active, innovative participation by the people.

Third, the pattern of interactions during the history of development produced a "charmed loop" (Cronen et al. 1982) for the planners. See Figure 5.2. Perhaps the most interesting aspect of this model is that it depicts no possible pattern of reflexive effects that would achieve the goal of decentralization. In this pattern of social reality, no matter what the masses did, the planners would interpret this as a mandate for their continued work. The centralized agency might diminish or increase in influence relative to the masses, but it is never about to wither away.

The loop is formed by three factors. 1) The sequence envisions a change produced in the masses by the skillful and efficacious activities of the planners. Because of the development programs, the masses are expected to take on the features by which they are perceived in the planners' "romantic" rather than "realistic" perceptions. The important aspect of this change is the attribution of responsibility; the masses' "improvement" is

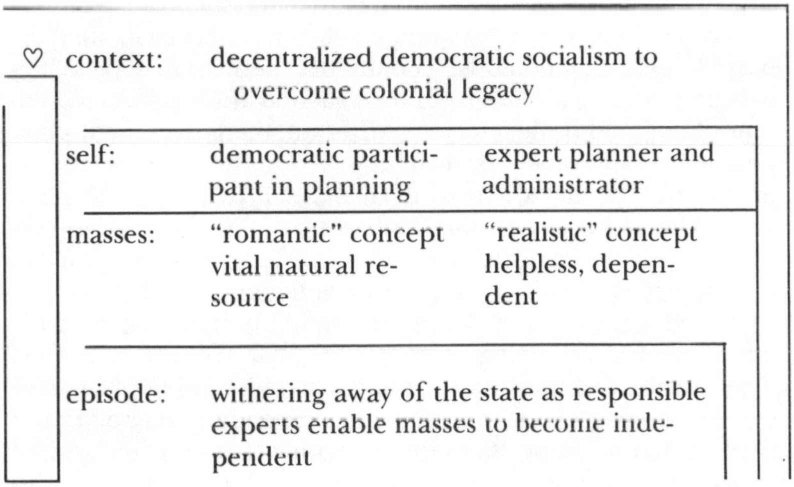

♡ context:	decentralized democratic socialism to overcome colonial legacy	
self:	democratic participant in planning	expert planner and administrator
masses:	"romantic" concept vital natural resource	"realistic" concept helpless, dependent
episode:	withering away of the state as responsible experts enable masses to become independent	

Figure 5.2. Planners' "charmed loop" of perpetual responsibility.

the result of the professional activity of the planners, for which they are prepared to take the credit or blame. 2) The strong commitment to democratic institutions implies that there is a limit to the amount of "blame" that can be placed on the masses. The "romantic" perception of the masses is not only a residue of the rhetoric in which the nation was formed, it is a necessary constituent of any democratic process of development. The "pragmatic" issue described above implies that development cannot occur (unless by force) unless the masses choose to adopt innovations, and these choices will not be made unless they perceive these products or activities as relevant to their felt needs. 3) The planners' commitment to community development integrates it with other national programs. They believe that neither community development nor other projects can prosper alone.

These factors produce an interesting pattern of reflexive effects. The professional self-concept of the planners as a centralized agency is reinforced no matter what happens.

If the masses became fully active, fulfilling the most romantic concept of their initiative in development, then the planners would see their role as continuing. They would coordinate (perhaps largely autonomous) community development activities with the other national programs, such as fiscal policy, regulation of national trade, etcetera. After all, the government planners are responsible for bringing about the changes in the masses that permit them to participate in decentralized planning. Therefore, a centralized office must be maintained to preclude losing the gains to the inroads of foreign aggression, international exploitation, or domestic inflation.

On the other hand, if the masses do not become active participants in development programs, the planners are to blame. Their professionalism, efficacy, and activities have not been sufficient to bring about the kind of change they intended, and they should increase their efforts with a better plan, and of course a continuing centralized agency should perform this function.

The effects of the development effort have beome matters of the public record, but whether these are seen as a smashing triumph or a failure depends on the perspective from which they are viewed. It is possible that the planners are unable to see the facts as constituting success. Not only do the achievements fall short of that which was desired, but if they perceived all their goals as met, they would have defined themselves as finished with a phase of their professional activities they prize.

Regardless of these "deeper" motivations for perceiving success, the planners have in fact consistently evaluated the results of their development plans as having fallen considerably short of the mark, and have blamed themselves—that is, the centralized bureacracy. In 1958, the evaluation chastized the extension agency for not giving adequate technical and other guidance for development programs, and blamed the administrators of the plan for poorly coordinating with nonofficial organizations and for not delegating implementation and planning to the people. The report wryly concluded that the people's movement is on but the people's representatives have yet to join it. In 1974, the lack of integration among the research, teaching and extension efforts for agricultural development was cited as a reason for the lack of results. The 20-point development strategy was an explicit assertion that the long-range plans were not having the desired impact on the people, and was an attempt to find another way that the centralized bureaucracy could have the effects it desired.

Given the social reality of the planners, there is no exit from this charmed loop. The logic of these social realities impels them to act, and any consequence of their actions is perceived as reinforcing their role as a strongly centralized agency. In one way, the planners are the best available examples of modernity, with a constant quest to change one's own—and other people's—mind about virtually any topic. Paralleling the incessant quest for innovation in modernity, whatever pattern of events occurs in the interactions among agents in development, the planners will interpret them as a call for their own renewed efforts.

The Social Reality of Change Agents

THE GOVERNMENT SET ITSELF a difficult national goal: achieving material prosperity within the limits of power and procedure imposed by democratic institutions. There were monumental physical and economic obstacles, made more difficult by the self-imposed restrictions of democratic processes and socialist objectives. As part of the development effort, the government created a bureaucracy to serve as an intermediary between masses and planners. This decision had much greater effect than was expected, in part because it institutionalized the tensions produced by the incompatible roles embraced by a strong central government seeking to decentralize development activities.

This bureaucracy had a dual responsibility. On the one hand, it represented at the local level the central government's determination to initiate profound changes in the traditional philosophy, social structure, and economic ways of life. On the other, it served as a means of two-way communication between the planners and the masses, initiating an egalitarian partnership in a national people's movement of development. These two roles are not commensurate, and their incompatibility produced an unresolved tension, currently manifested as two dilemmas in which the development bureaucracy's change agents are caught.

THE BUREAUCRACY OF DEVELOPMENT

It has long been recognized that if any aspects of the government's goals are to be realized, public administration must function effectively and have the confidence of the people. One (but only one) standard for the successful functioning of public administration is the capabilities of its personnel. Various organizational structures affect the activities of the individuals who work in them. A "bad" organization can frustrate the attempts of competent individuals to act competently, and a "good" organization can make very effective the acts of persons of modest capabilities. However, it is not likely that a new organization, entrusted with such a difficult task as development, can succeed if its personnel do not have a sufficient degree of "administrative capability."

In general, capable administrators are defined as those who possess desirable traits such as awareness of the organization's goals and mission; ability to set and achieve performance goals; appropriate attitudes, behavior, and motivation; and, perhaps most important, a perception of themselves as efficacious.

The role and structure of the development bureaucracy has changed during the development history in India. Administration has become more complex and demanding, as a function of (1) the necessity to accomplish development objectives with relatively scarce resources; (2) the differences in the social realities of the administrators and the masses; (3) the masses' demands that the government supply their needs; and (4) the difficulty in eliciting intelligent and meaningful public cooperation from an uneducated public largely indifferent to the government.

The traditional social structure in India did not feature close ties between the government and the local communities. This in itself posed a problem for development, because the masses' perception of a government always determines the legitimacy of its activities. If this legitimacy is lacking, the masses respond apathetically to exhortations and withdraw from invitations to participate in national activities. Apathy and withdrawal are, of course, antithetical to development success.

Since Independence, the responsibility for increasing contact between the masses and the government has rested with the change agents. The goal has been to make the government work not only *for* the people but *with* the people, to enlist the people as active citizens.

The quality of the interaction between the citizens and government is thought to determine the amount of development that occurs. A number of theorists and public administrators assume that the achievement of development goals depends on the success of the development bureaucracy in getting the masses involved in development projects in cooperation with the government. The function of the development bureaucracy is to maintain a circular process starting from the formulation of policy, continuing through implementation and modification on the basis of the results, and back to policy formulation again.

Change agents mobilize, allocate, and combine the actions that are technically needed to achieve development objectives. Katz (1969) termed this ability "administrative capability" and suggested three "appraisal contours": ability to effect intended results in terms of present and past performance, linkages with the environment, and the organizational and guidance structure of the administration.

The ability to perform effectively derives from the image people have of the development bureaucracy. In a process of communication such as change agents are charged to perform, the administration must both be and be perceived as a reliable channel between government and the masses. Among other things, this requires some measure of trust that the change agents are capable and unbiased.

Linkages with the environment suggests appraisal of the agency's ability to obtain and deliver the physical and economic resources involved in the development effort, and the extent to which it is informed and in coordination with other groups. Among other things, this appraisal contour requires the perception that the agency is efficacious.

There is good evidence that the development bureaucracy has not achieved a high level of administrative capability according to Katz's appraisal contours. Further, the change agents themselves believe they do not show well in these appraisals; they display a varied but predominantly low level of professional self-esteem and motivation. This discontent itself undercuts the image and efficacy of the organization. Organizing a development bureaucracy has posed a problem for all developing nations. Narula (1969) argued that administrative structures deriving from colonial rule were not well suited to the specific demands of development, and new agencies had to be created. The underlying philosophy for these new agencies was operational autonomy, insulation from political pressures, and provision for the participation of clientele groups in the formulation and implementation of policies. The paramount obstacles to effective functioning of these organizations are the nonparticipation or inadequate participation of the clientele groups; the lack of continuous two-way communication between the field and the secretariat; and the presence among administrators of values, attitudes, and motivations among administrators not conducive to effective action.

Narula (1971) concluded that the administration of development programs must be dynamic in order to adjust to changing contexts (such as population growth and industrialization), and to the effects of development activities themselves. For example, every five-year plan, he argued, should be accompanied by a "counterpart plan" of administrative development and change, making the structure of the development bureaucracy commensurate with the rationale and materials of current programs.

The requirement of administering the Indian development program would stagger any organization. During the course of the development effort, a number of modernizations have been implemented in its administrative systems and procedures, but there has been no basic change in the overall patterns of personnel management or administrative structure. A number of projects conducted in the 1970s by study teams of the Administrative Reforms Commission suggested that five factors constrain the efficacy of development administrative performance: (1) lack of specific knowledge and experience in administering a development program; (2) low morale and inadequate motivation; (3) insufficient promotional incentives for improving performance; (4) inadequate commitment among the civil servants for achieving results in the field; (5) bureaucratic values, attitudes and practices steeped in the "law and order" tradition of government.

Our research indicates that low morale, motivation, and commitment are not characteristics people bring to their tasks as change agents. Rather, they arise from patterns of interactions within the government and between the change agents and the masses. The structure of the dialogue is such as to place change agents in a bind that necessarily makes them inefficacious; they must act, but all acts available to them are invalidated.

CHANGE AGENTS

We found it useful to differentiate "administrative" from "contact" change agents. Contact agents participate in daily interactions with the masses. They consist of block development officers, village-level workers, panchyat secretaries, and pradhan (elected opinion leaders)—and, in the Jhangirpuri area, Delhi Development Authority officers. Block development officers are supposed to visit villages in their block at least once a week and more frequently during an intense development campaign. Village-level workers are expected to be in the village daily, panchyat secretaries two or three times a week, and pradhans live in their village. Delhi Development Authority representatives are supposed to be in their offices daily.

Administrative agents include development program specialists and the functional heads of various facilities involved in development projects, such as water, sewerage, public transit, and health care. Project heads come into contact with the masses through other agents, not directly; program specialists meet the masses during special campaigns, but much less frequently than contact agents.

We did a study of fifteen change agents, all of whom worked either with Lampur or Jhangirpuri residents. Eight of the change agents were "administrative" agents, seven were "contact" agents. A semistructured interview schedule was used to elicit their development orientation, participation, and motivation. All were interviewed personally. Contact agents were interviewed in Hindi (the local language), administrative agents in English. Verbal responses to open-ended questions were recorded and later content-analyzed. Of particular value was the notion of identifying the subjects' interpretive contexts and the relations among the levels of contexts.

THE CONTEXTS OF CHANGE AGENTS' SOCIAL REALITY

The social reality of change agents can be described in terms of three levels of contexts. The most encompassing context is the socioeconomic programs in general. These include programs of health care and public facilities, public transit and agricultural development. At the second level are particular relationships and arenas for action, including interactions with panchyats and village leaders, people's development participation, local development strategies, and administrative decisions. At the third and most specific level of contexts are particular episodes: cleaning of community latrines and garbage removal; destruction, through vandalism or neglect, of government-provided facilities such as hydrants and street lights, and then demanding their replacement; distribution to the landless of agricultural land acquired under the Land Ceiling Act; malfunctioning of medical facilities due to political pressures and unavailability of medical and paramedical staff; the village pond as a source of health hazard; overcrowded public buses; gherao (mass demonstrations outside change agents' offices).

PERCEPTIONS OF SELF AND OTHER DEVELOPMENT AGENTS

In addition to these contexts, the social realities of the change agents include important professional and personal self-concepts, and a particular perception of the masses.

Self-Concept

Change agents have a concept of what development is supposed to achieve, how the process should go, and their role in it. The self-perceived efficacy of development functionaries derives from the quality of their interaction with the masses, from increasing their professional and personal capabilities, from their status within the development bureaucracy, and from their success in administering particular programs.

We interpret our research data as indicating that the change agents see themselves as the point of contact between government and people, charged with bringing the materials of development to the people and eliciting the active, cooperative participation of the people in the continuing, self-sustaining process of development. This is an intensely personal position, in which concepts of self are involved. For the contact agents, their self-concepts are bound up with interpersonal relationships with the masses; the personal and professional identities of administrative agents are invested in particular facilities and services.

More blatantly than any of our subjects themselves, we summarize their professional self-concept in this way: They see themselves as the efficacious dispensers of scarce government commodities to a grateful public who will respond by responsibly caring for those commodities, actively participating in development programs, and taking initiative in identifying needs and designing programs to meet those needs.

Their concept of self—and of how the process of development should proceed—contains a number of perceptions and beliefs that are threatened by the existing patterns of interaction with the masses and within the bureaucracy.

ADMINISTRATIVE CHANGE AGENTS. Personal and professional self-concepts are usefully differentiated.

Professional self. Several institutional factors facilitate development of the change agents' professional self concept. Administrators need to be well informed about on-going development activities. Multi-directional orientation programs are arranged periodically to bring them up to date on development information. Agency or project heads are oriented by field evaluation studies and by the concerned departments; planning officers are oriented by group meetings and discussions with functional heads; lower-level functionaries are preoriented by functional heads, intermediate-level functionaries, field evaluation studies, and the masses themselves.

Despite these orientation meetings, administrative change agents believe they are not adequately motivated to deal with the public. Therefore, they feel it is necessary to organize motivation training camps for themselves and for other levels of personnel in the development bureaucracy.

Their own motivation to participate is rooted in the motivation of the masses: when the masses seem uninterested, this disheartens the administrators. When there is effective interpersonal communication at all levels, from the grassroots to the highest levels, the agents are more motivated to participate in development programs. A spirit of public service and of duty consciousness—of total involvement in the development task—helps to develop their professional self.

The most important motivational component of their self-concept is their feeling that they are effective. Our subjects cited several activities that give them a sense of professional efficacy. Training lower-level functionaries to handle development information and problems brings a sense of accomplishment. To facilitate adequate communication, the administrative change agents give the contact agents full information about localized problems, and train them to disseminate information and discern local problems, as well as act on the feedback given by the people through mass meetings, broadcasting forums, and program specialists. When the administrative change agents are in direct personal contact in mass meetings, radio, and television forums, they make people aware of innovations, development problems, and solutions.

Change agents feel effective in offering need-based programs if they have more frequent and periodic reviews and discussions with higher-level functionaries about failures and successes of ongoing programs. They also feel effective when they have executive powers. Our subjects who dealt with local development problems, particularly agriculture, felt their programs were administered well: problem-solving actions are taken speedily, technical guidance is provided in the village itself, and training and visit schemes to special project areas for specialized training are implemented.

Our subjects who were responsible for public transit service were less confident of their success. They described their efforts in conducting public opinion surveys, redressing public grievances, spot-checking if remedial measures are operative, and assessing cost effectiveness of new routes. However, they noted that public cooperation and awareness are also needed to make transit services efficient, and they perceived a need to educate the public how to utilize services for safe and speedy travel. They blamed both mass media and interpersonal channels for failing to provide this education, and criticized the operating staff as lacking a spirit of public service and duty consciousness.

An enduring problem for all change agents is the ratio between resources and need. The financial and physical resources to which they have access are far less than required; they always have to choose among deserving projects, leaving important things undone.

More than the sheer size of the task, however, they feel that the quality of their interactions with the masses and with other components of the bureaucracy make them ineffective and sap their motivation. They do not like the pattern of their interactions with the planners. As shown in Figure 6.1, they perceive themselves as limited by the way they are treated by planners and by the functionaries in the other agencies with with they have to work. The planners, they feel, give them too little power and autonomy to implement their projects. Often the administrators are forced to give priorities to particular projects and localities because someone in the bureaucracy has succumbed to political pressures or has a vested interest other than meeting the need of the area. They blame the multiagencies for improper implementation of projects because of bureaucratic delays, undue interference, and poorly planned and uncoordinated action among the agencies.

This feeling of impotence is exacerbated by their interactions with the masses. The administrative change agents blame the masses for the failure of development projects, citing their passive participation. The pattern of actions and attributions made by the administrative change agents is shown in Figure 6.2.

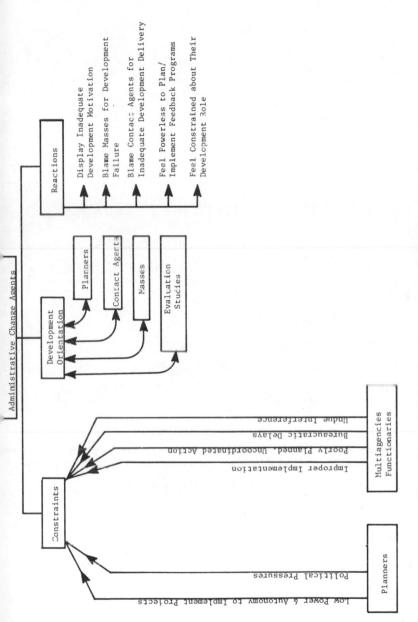

Figure 6.1. Administrative change agents' interaction with planners.

Administrative Change Agents

Reactions

Display Inadequate
Development Motivation

Blame Masses for Development
Failure

Blame Contact Agents for
Inadequate Development Delivery

Feel Powerless to Plan/
Implement Feedback Programs

Feel Constrained about Their
Development Role

Development Orientation

Planners

Contact Agents

Masses

Evaluation Studies

Constraints

Multiagencies Functionaries

Undue Interference

Bureaucratic Delays

Poorly Planned, Uncoordinated Action

Improper Implementation

Planners

Political Pressures

Low Power & Autonomy to Implement Projects

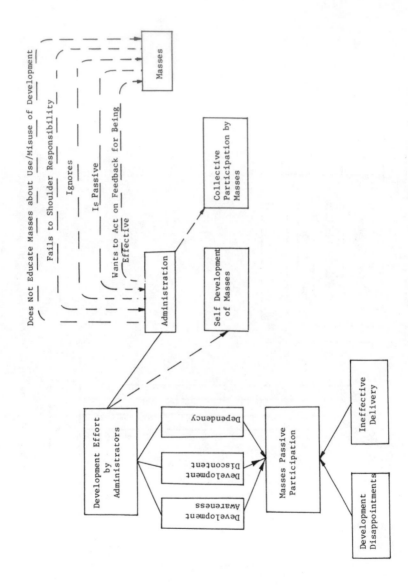

Figure 6.2. Administrative change agents' interaction with masses.

The interaction can be illustrated by continuing the example of the tap water project. The administrative change agents see the project as originating with themselves. They perceive the need first and then inform the masses about the brackishness of the water from tubewells and the threat it poses. The masses' desire for taps in or close to their homes is the result of the administrators' educational and communicative efforts.

Instead of gratitude and respect, however, the masses respond to the initiative of the change agents by resenting and criticizing them. The people argue that since the change agents are not capable of providing taps immediately, and probably never providing all of the taps desired, then it was unnecessary and undesirable to make them aware of the problem with tubewells in the first place.

The change agents see this response as passive and dependent, not taking into consideration their own limited resources. While they are able and willing to provide technical advice and material if the masses are willing to contribute labor and time, they can by themselves neither provide all the desired taps unilaterally nor synchronize "awareness of need" and the "delivery of goods and services."

The combination of these interaction patterns creates a debilitating sense of inefficacy. For example, the agents may oppose or simply not do much about tap water projects. To the extent they are successful in creating discontent and development awareness, they are perceived as powerless to meet the need and resented for arousing awareness of it. Further, their attempt to implement the tap water project makes them confront their own powerlessness in interactions with the masses and with planners and the multiagencies.

The agents are better off if they do nothing. Only then can they escape situations that undeniably demonstrate their ineffectiveness. But if they aggressively pursue the tap water project, they will be unable to deliver the new taps, because the masses will not take an active participatory role and because the planners and multiagencies are inefficient, uncoordinated, and subject to political pressures.

Our subjects reported that they have opposed poorly conceived programs and have in fact tried to block programs that pander to vested interests; but they also reported little success. The best they can do is to go along grudgingly, and this disillusions them with development and undercuts their professional self-concept.

Change agents, especially those dealing with agricultural programs, believe that implementation strategies are poorly planned and ineffectively coordinated. They lodge three specific criticisms: Base-line surveys and research are not utilized; the local people are not consulted when local strategies are planned; and many irrelevant plans are started because of vested interests and are terminated midway when it has become obvious they are not realistic. Agricultural program specialists believe that implementation strategies are unrealistic because administrative generalists do not delegate any executive power—particularly in control of the budget—to specialists. Moreover, inordinate bureaucratic delays affect the time-bound operations of development programs, and the coordination of activities is thwarted by the multiagency involvement without any one designated as responsible for the effectiveness of the programs. The delays result from the present block development structures and other administrative agencies in which there are too many levels of hierarchy involved in every development program decision. Unrealistic planning not only wastes scarce government resources but makes the administrative change agents ineffective in implementing the programs.

As shown in Figure 6.2, there is a complex and by now familiar pattern of interaction between the administrators and the masses. The administrators are frustrated because they do not have adequate resources to provide all the services the masses need. This combination of assumed responsibility, inadequate provision of services, and expressed frustration elicits a complex response by the masses, including a high degree of development awareness, discontent, and dependency. Figure 6.2 shows this as a rapid, reiterated cycle of exchanges in which each blames the other. Administrators cite the masses' passivity as a reason for their own discouragement and selective expenditure of resources; the masses cite the administrators' unresponsiveness and their failure to discharge their responsibility as the justification for their own unwillingness to invest their time and initiative in development projects.

Public transit administrators are aware of people's problems and demands. They would like to meet these demands without delay, but cannot since they do not have enough funds. The problem is made worse because the rurban resettlement colonies expand in size without coordination between the housing and public transit agencies.

Health care administrators are concerned about providing good health care facilities at the medical centers in the villages and conurbation colonies—that is, providing an adequate number of doctors and paramedical staff and quality medicine. But they feel helpless for several reasons. Not many medical doctors and paramedical staff are ready to serve outside urban centers where they would lack basic living comforts; and the concept of doctors commuting to their place of work has not developed, nor is it convenient or cost effective in the prevailing situations.

The lack of personnel, even more than problems of funding, is the major impediment in providing adequate health facilities. Also, the quality of medicine is poor in part because of widespread corruption and the assumption that people will cheat and steal. For example, the doctors accuse the paramedics of diluting medicines with water and selling the rest.

The masses' social structure and their action patterns cause problems for the effective delivery of medical services. In one instance, high-caste villagers boycotted a medical center because water to be used in medical practices had been brought to the center by low-caste persons. In another, high-caste persons refused to rent a building they owned for the government to use for medical centers because low-caste persons would be treated in it. Other constraining factors include political pressures and community factions. Political office holders often demand that regardless of need facilities be provided in areas they favor. High-caste persons often demand exclusive facilities for them in conurbation complexes. Sometimes people become discontent with medical services and taunt, threaten, even attack doctors and paramedic staff.

Administrators feel they have been more successful in creating a desire for health care among the masses than in making them aware of solutions to day-to-day environmental health hazards. They have been effective in making the masses conscious of the need for safe drinking water in the villages but not in providing safe water quickly. In deciding where to lay pipe for water connections, many administrators deliberately give priority to those villages that are self-reliant and that contribute physical labor and money, even though these may not be the villages where the need is greatest.

The administrators perceive themselves as not making sufficient efforts to educate the public about the use and misuse of the amenities they are able to provide. Running water hydrants are a common sight in conurbation colonies even though water is scarce. They also see themselves as inadequately teaching people how to maintain the facilities, such as keeping overhead tanks clean and desilting water pipes. If the public is educated in this respect and if they cooperate, then the amount of money and time otherwise spent in maintaining these facilities can be used to provide facilities to a greater number of people. The administrators complain that a facility they provide must be paid for thrice: the original cost, the cost of repairing it when broken, the cost of replacing it when stolen.

Administrators feel that programs become increasingly unrelated to the needs of the people because during the course of their operation there is insufficient research to evaluate their impact. Research is used to design programs but not to monitor them.

Administrators feel their expression of their professional self is limited by the system in which they work. They often find themselves in a situation where they have made a promise to meet a particular need and have the resources to meet that need, but they cannot fulfill their promise because the delivery system is inadequate. For example, they are sometimes frustrated by the social structure of the villages. Not only the ratio of resources to needs but the objective of self-sustaining development implies that local cooperation is necessary for development objectives to be reached. This cooperation is often not available, in part because of the old matter of the village social structure. In short, the rural elites block the flow of information and material to the weaker sections of the society. See Figure 6.3. The government may offer incentives in the form of low interest loans or reduced prices for active participation in installing the capacity for tap water. However, the elites—who are most likely to learn about these incentives—often do not tell less privileged persons about them. This gives the elites greater opportunity to take advantage of the incentives for themselves. Since the elites often control the community television set, they can block the poorer people's access to information by turning off the receiver. The elites often meet the visiting development officials and give them incorrect information about the village and pass on to the poor distorted reports of the government's offers.

Their dependence on the local social structure undermines the administrators' concept of themselves as professionally effective, and this reduces their morale.

The village panchyats are set up by the government to provide autonomy and administrative leadership to the villages, but this innovation has not been fully effective. Although they are elected by the community, the panchyats are not necessarily community-oriented; rather, their decisions are often governed by vested interests. Because of the growing feeling among the masses that the village panchyats have become corrupt and are reflecting only their own vested interests or narrow village factions, the people are fast losing faith in their own representatives and are less willing to take responsibility for development. In summary, the panchyats no longer remain a democratic forum for village participation.

Personal self. Development awareness, motivation, and the people's faith is necessary to give personal pride to administrators who want to help the masses develop. But personally they find themselves helpless because the public is not cooperative, they are dependent on ineffective local social structures, they

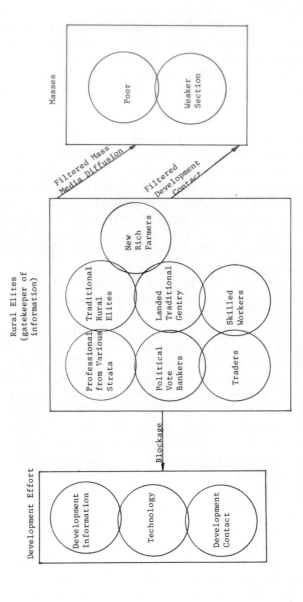

Figure 6.3. Rural elites: filters of development efforts.

are denied influence and autonomy by the bureaucratic administrative structure, and their status and credit is incommensurate with their contribution to development activities. They are disheartened and frustrated because they feel ineffective and because professional rewards and punishments are distributed capriciously or on the basis of reasons other than merit.

CONTACT CHANGE AGENTS. *Professional self.* Contact change agents believe they can enhance their professional self by being aware of local development activities and problems and by involvement in development projects. Their awareness of development activities and problems comes from contacts with higher-level administrators in regular meetings, discussions, and reviews. During these meetings, not only do they get an awareness of the local areas assigned to them but also of the neighboring areas as representatives from these areas express their awareness, experience, and problems. Development awareness is also created by personal contacts with the villagers and through regular meetings of the opinion leaders in the agent's assigned block meetings of the opinion leaders in the agent's assigned block villages.

Our subjects were keenly aware of the limits of their power to redress the grievances of the masses or to convey the people's feedback about development to higher-level administrators.

Contact agents cooperate with multiprogram agencies by soliciting public cooperation in development campaigns and organizing motivational camps in villages for facilitating adoption of innovations. The higher authorities also orient them as to what local programs should be initiated and how to perform the IEC (information, education, communication) functions. The action program targets are given out by the higher authorities. The agents' participation in group meetings with colleagues from block villages and with higher authorities also help in finding solutions for localized problems and for ways of implementing programs.

Inadequate equipment and supplies prevent contact change agents from performing effectively. Officers hired by the Field Publicity Unit to show documentary and news films in the villages have an inadequate number of vans that serve as mobile theaters. Even with full utilization of equipment, they may get to particular villages as infrequently as once a year. Village-level workers complain that they often cannot obtain audiotape recorders or cassettes to record the radio and teleclub discussions. "Barefoot community health workers" were trained to provide immediate health care to the villagers. Their training was expensive and lasted half a year, but the medicines and bandages they used while ministering to ill people were not replaced. Out of supplies, they quickly became helpless, and the program soon became ineffective.

The contact agents in our study were not happy about their role in development. They feel that higher-level administrators do not give adequate guidance for implementing programs or for redressing grievances.

The contact agents feel unable to improve local communities' communication with the central government. Even when they are able to provide community communication facilities, such as television sets or radios, these devices are placed in private houses and monopolized by a few elites.

The contact agents' interactions with their administrators and with the masses are unsatisfactory. They sense they are not trusted to do a proper job, and they feel the people perceive them as helpless. As shown in Figure 6.4, contact change agents are very much in the middle of a complex network of interactions.

Consider again the tap water project. In interaction with the masses and/or higher levels of the development bureaucracy, the contact change agent may be sensitized to the issue. If he hears of it from complaints by the masses about brackish water or the difficulty of travel to a water source, it is his job to demand exclusive facilities to bring change. On the other hand, if he hears of it from the administrator of a project, it is his duty to inform the masses. Either way, the contact change agent is identified with the issue, since he is the one who brought the "news" of it. He is not authorized to provide the taps needed to solve the problem. However, he is blamed by the masses for the failure

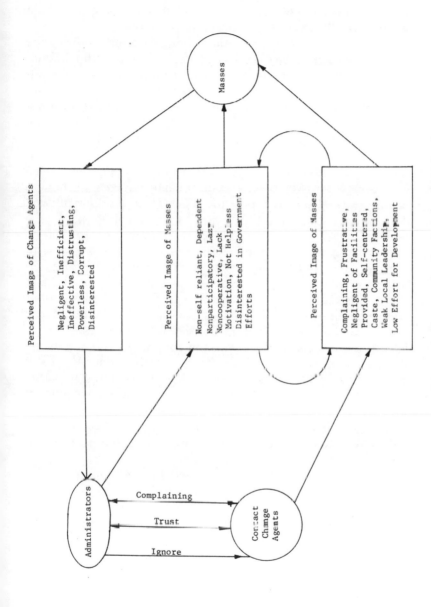

Figure 6.4. Communication gap for development participation.

of the government to deliver taps or blamed by the government for the unwillingness of the masses to cooperate.

Such interactions make contact change agents confront the fact that they have limited information and less authority, and this reduces their credibility both with the masses and the administrators. Our subjects responded to this situation by blaming both administrators and the masses, accusing the administrators of having little administrative capability (although not using this term) and the masses of being discouraged and selfish.

The two groups of change agents perceive the masses' participation very differently. Where administrative change agents believe the masses to be passive, contact change agents see them as having learned not to expect too much from the government. The contact agents see the masses as participating actively by making themselves better informed, by asking for information, by clarifying things they do not understand, by offering solutions and feedback about ongoing activities, by demanding new development activities as solutions to immediate needs, and more. But the people's enthusiasm wanes when their solutions and suggestions are not taken into account, when their demands are not met, and when their grievances are not redressed. They have come to believe that contact agents have no power to redress grievances and administrators are indifferent. All of this amounts to what the masses take as a valid reason to stop participating actively. As a result, the masses only adopt development practices that are in their immediate self-interest.

At times, villagers are willing to solve their own problems, but only when they have to make no direct contribution in labor, cash, or kind. They feel the government has the responsibility to provide them with what they need for development. This marks a change over the course of the development decades. Twenty years ago in what are considered "progressive villages," the masses were willing to contribute at least labor, but now they have shifted total responsibility to the government. The rural elites are unwilling to contribute disproportionate amounts toward the common good, and the have-nots are unwilling to contribute at all because they are striving hard for immediate survival. And the low degree of public participation that is available often fails due to ineffective local leadership, ineffective communication policies, and sluggish motivation. Figure 6.5 summarizes some of the reasons why the masses lack strong initiative to participate in development.

The necessity of community initiative and the unwillingness of the masses to provide it places the government in a dilemma. On the one hand, the masses want speedy development and the government promises speedy development for all, but on the other hand, government has limited resources and the masses do not want to commit their resources for development. When asked to suggest and become a part of solutions for their problems, the masses instead offer complaints about the existing and operating development programs. They do not acknowledge the limitations of the government.

Disheartened by the lack of success in many projects, contact change agents insist they are not fully responsible and that the masses must share the burden. But there is poor communication among the administrators, contact agents, and the masses on this point. The change agents have never made a constructive effort to explain to the masses the limitations of government resources and of the agents' own authority. Their reluctance stems, in part, from their unwillingness to acknowledge—much less "confess"—their failure to attain their professional self-concept. The administrators and contact agents both tend to grumble and complain to each other about limited resources and authority. Ironically, their unacknowledged limitations are quite apparent to the masses. The result of this pattern of poor communication is that failures or delays in meeting the masses' demands are not explained, and promises that the masses are being heard and will be responded to by development programs are not persuasive.

The change agents realize that interpersonal communication with the people is necessary for need-based programs. They believe that direct contact with the masses helps them in planning for these programs and in redressing their grievances. In the past, they depended on indirect feedback about the masses'

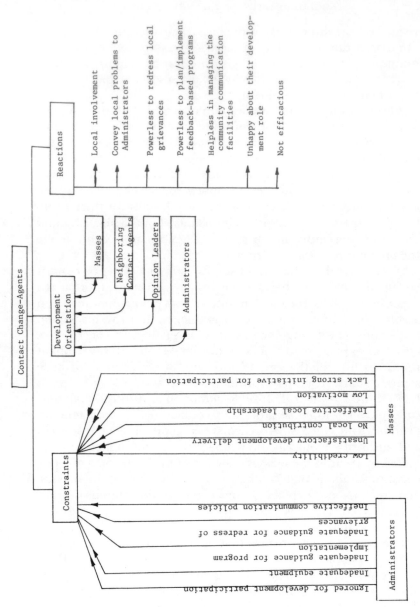

Figure 6.5. Contact change agents' development interaction with ad-

development needs through traditional opinion leaders and leader bridges, but that is no longer sufficient; they seek more frequent contact directly with the people.

Personal Self. Contact change agents feel they have lost personal credibility with the masses. Because they are not effective in redressing the masses' grievances, the people accuse them of corruption and malpractices—for example, diverting government resources to themselves or their favored groups. But actually the contact agents find themselves helpless because they are ignored by administrators and are not given sufficient information about future plans or sufficient executive power to satisfy queries and demands from the public. This mistrust is particularly debilitating for their development motivation and self-concept because it results from a pattern of interaction initiated by their own effective action in making the masses or the administrators aware of a development need. After awhile, they learn not to be too aggressive in identifying needs.

The only persons who express confidence and trust in the village-level workers, the panchyat secretaries, and opinion leaders are the block development officers. This trust is an important personal motivation for them to involve themselves in development tasks.

Perception of the Masses

The interactions between masses and change agents are affected by the way each group perceives the other. These perceptions comprise the context in which the other's actions are interpreted, and which guide subsequent acts.

ADMINISTRATIVE CHANGE AGENTS. Administrators expect the masses to participate in development, to be self-reliant, and to be cooperative. But they perceive that the masses actually are passive participants and not actively involved in implementing development. They are dependent, lazy, demanding, nonself-reliant and non-cooperative; but not as helpless as they used to be. At present, masses are very development aware, ready to accept and adopt development practices, but very discontented with administrators' development efforts because they are not receiving as many goods and services as they want.

The administrators explain the masses' development behavior on the basis of a particular model of Indian rural and rurban society. While this model is more implicit than explicit, its dimensions can be ascertained by the willingness of the administrators to make—and accept—certain attributions of motives. This model envisions a sequence from initial fatalism to development awareness, discontent and then active participation. Interruptions or deviations from this sequence are seen as the result of operant conditioning. Specifically, they see the masses as realizing that they are not as helpless as they once thought they were but as having learned to be dependent on the government. This learned dependency produces passive participation.

Development Awareness. Administrators perceive masses as highly aware of development programs and ready to accept change per se and adopt specific innovations. They are psychologically aroused to feel the need for more and better development facilities, such as better medical facilities, agricultural innovations, and safe drinking water. The two factors that facilite readiness to accept innovation are exposure to urbanization—a model which makes them aspire to a better life—and the communication network of mass media and interpersonal channels—which informs them about innovative ways to do things.

Though the masses are highly development aware, the administrators feel they have to make additional efforts to motivate the masses for self-development and collective participation in development.

Development Discontent. Administrators perceive the masses as discontented about failures to achieve the goals of development, and specifically about the failure of the administrators themselves in delivering services and goods to them. They attribute their unanswered demands to inefficient delivery systems in the administration of development and explain the inefficiency as the result of administrators who do not respond to the masses' demands and criticisms. As the administrators perceive it, the masses have a concept of the administrators as disinterested and the contact agents as powerless. The masses allege that the administrators block information to the weaker sections of the people because of their vested interest in the elite section of the society, and give very little authority to exercise power to the contact agents who are in a position to redress their day-to-day complaints.

Administrators feel that masses have a point in saying that their grievences are not redressed speedily even if these are conveyed verbally or in writing to the administrators. As a result, people feel ignored by the administrators and get the feeling that administrators are indifferent to their development as well as to their participation in development. They also feel that is why they are not included in future development plans of their own localities.

One expression of the masses' discontent involves land acquisition under the Agricultural Land Ceiling Act. Under this act, the government took land away from large landholders in an attempt to redistribute the sources of wealth. However, in many instances, nothing has been done with the land: It lies unused and useless to everyone, a daily reminder of the government's failure to deliver on its promises. The development intentions of the government may have been noble and genuine, but the administrative delays in redistributing the land has dismayed the public.

The public transit system provided by the government is another source of the public's discontent. Administrators believe that people are discontented not only because of inefficient operation but because the administrators concerned with this program are rude and negligent in dealing with the public.

Development Participation. Administrators believe that the masses do not participate actively in implementing development programs. At best, masses only adopt development practices, whereas the administrators want them to engage in active participation because only this serves objective of self-sustaining development. To be sure, the initial development programs took the form of handouts, but these should yield in time to projects expressing local initiative in a sequence in which development is restructured by being tailored to local needs. This restructuring entails an involvement of the local people in the search for solutions and strategies, and then acting on them.

The weaker sections do not participate at all because they feel neglected in the content and form of development programs and unwanted and unrespected by administrators, contact agents, local elites and higher castes (in villages). Moreover, the poorest sections of local communities are not sufficiently assertive to overcome the barriers that the social structure places on their active participation in development. Government efforts to by-pass this structure are not usually successful, because the government's resources are themselves limited. On the other hand, the local elites have learned to be dependent on the government and are unwilling to make sacrifices—or expend efforts—that will benefit all equally.

As perceived by the administrators, the masses are insatiable. Everything that the government does for the masses simply teaches them to want more and to be more dependent on the government. In one sense, the more they do for the masses, the farther away they push the goal of self-sustaining development. But since the government has committed itself to provide the infrastructure for development and to raise the material well-being of the people, the administrators try to meet the people's demands—knowing they will fail in the attempt—until they become terminally disillusioned with their role in development.

CONTACT CHANGE AGENTS. The contact agents perceive the masses as uncooperative in community development efforts due to community factions, castes, and greater concern for individual than community gain. They feel that the present educational system encourages an individualistic orientation characterized by selfish and self-centered behavior. These forms of behavior lead to the disintegration of opinion leadership, whether elected or traditional, in the villages. Without some form of effective leadership, the villages are unable to work collectively in cooperation with development efforts.

Moreover, the individualistic pattern makes the masses hesitant to put forth sufficient effort for development. They raise questions such as these: Is our effort commensurable with the benefits to be gained? Are we putting forth more effort than others in the community? Is the community's effort commensurate with that by the government? The process itself of raising these questions itself delays and impedes participation, and the forms in which the questions are posed preclude working for the common good rather than one's own interests.

Like the administrators, contact agents are disturbed by the masses' negligent handling and misuse of the facilities provided by the government. As a result of abuse, people are deprived of the use of these facilities until the government can allocate sufficient resources to replace them. Much of the development "need" is suffering that results directly from the people's own irresponsible behavior. In the urban slum areas, instead of cooperating with the contact agents—e.g., the medical staff, the Delhi Development Authority officers—the majority of the people harass them and hold them responsible for the lack of adequate facilities. Since urban slums are not cohesive communities, there are few social controls to moderate the actions of the rowdy elements. Frustrated by a life of greater want than is found in rural communities, urban slum dwellers use violent tactics to obtain the services they want. For example, in Jhangirpuri, they have a history of threatening paramedical staff and doctors with knives to get medicines and treatments.

The contact agents are angry with the masses' utter disregard for the facilities they have been provided and for hindering development activites by irresponsible behavior. For example, the government has particularly focused its efforts on the socially downtrodden harijan class (the sweepers, the scavengers, the lowest caste). Harijans are better off now than they have ever been because of the government's programs of direct action, legislation, and education. This class is now conscious of their rights and has access to all development programs. But instead of gratitude or even sullen cooperation, the harijans are creating social problems. As the story was told in chapter 2, they have become too grand to do menial work for each other. In Jhangirpuri, they refuse to collect garbage for persons of their own class even though they are hired by the DDA to do so. These low-caste people use strong measures to inform the government of their social rights, but they do not want to discharge the occupational duties assigned to them. The government is willing to help weaker sections by providing them with extra amenities, but contact agents believe that in return these sectors of the society should be prepared to make themselves socially useful.

The masses are perceived as corrupt. The government gives them cash subsidies and loans for various development projects, but they misuse these benefits while complaining that the government does not do anything for them. Contact agents see the people as having become lazy and dependent because the government has spoon-fed them in many development programs. They lack the motivation to articulate their development needs or to take steps to achieve those needs. But government has committed itself to the welfare of the masses, so it tries its best to provide need-based programs whether the masses demand them or not.

Here is the problem as the contact agents see it: As time passes, the masses are becoming more and more dependent on the government, making development more of the government's concern, responsibility, and duty. At present, they are so dependent that they will not so much as fill a deep pit in the middle of the road however much they may suffer from it. They complain and wait until government personnel come to fill it. Twenty years previously, these masses were very enthusiastic to share the development burden and contribute their labor. The puzzle is how and why this "backward transition" has taken place.

One of the answers may be that the masses have lost faith in the government development machinery due to bureaucratic delays. Most people can cite an example where the government has not kept what the masses understood to be its promise of delivering development speedily. The very poor in particular feel that their social position has worsened in the last twenty years and that social change and modernity have bypassed them.

Another suggestion is that the masses have learned to be dependent. Contact agents perceive development motivation as taking three steps. The people must perceive their own needs, articulate those needs as demands, and work through a strong local leadership to vocalize those demands as well as get them satisfied. They perceive the masses as having progressed through the first two steps but having failed miserably in the third. The result is a tragic lack of active participation at the local level. Figure 6.6 summarizes our discussion of the change agents' perception that the development programs themselves have produced an unwanted "learned dependency" that precludes self-sustaining development. Reading Figure 6.6 by columns from left to right, the original condition of rural Indians can be described as a fatalistic philosophy in a feudal social structure. On the individual level, they were content, dependent upon their community, unaware of alternative forms of life or ways of doing their daily tasks, and exploited by the elites. They thought of themselves in terms of their local community, neither as individuals with transcendent rights nor as members of some larger national political structure.

As shown in column 2, the government perceived all of these characteristics—except dependency to the local community—as problems to be alleviated. The government's intentions are shown in column 3: to improve the material quality of life, inform the people, emancipate them from exploitative linkages within the feudal social structure, and elicit their active participation in a national effort. At the same time, they wanted to work through the local community structure and therefore extolled the virtues and values of village life. In hindsight, these objectives are seen as not fully compatible.

Column 4 summarizes what the government actually did. It attempted to motivate the masses to seek and accept change, to educate them, to protect them from exploitation, and to develop channels of communication between the remotest village and the central government.

The actual effects of these activities were not always consonant with intentions. Column 5 shows that the government was successful in making the masses discontented, aware of innovations, informed about their personal rights and ready to insist on redress of past wrongs. However, it also produced a learned de-

1 FATALISM	2 CHARACTERIS- TICS PERCEIVED AS PROBLEMS	3 GOVERNMF INTENTIO
Contented	Yes	Improved quali life
Dependent	No	—
Unaware of inno- vations	Yes	Inform
Exploited	Yes	Emancipate
Participation lim- ited to the local social hierarchy	Yes	Develop self-aw ness as an indivi ual with rights a powers

*Figure 6.6. Hypothesis about the effects of development commur
tion programs.*

4 DEVELOPMENT EFFORTS	5 ACTUAL EFFECTS
ivate (e.g., create discon- ntment with things as ey are)	Discontent
—	Dependent on the government rather than on fate, land- lords, or social hierarchy
cate	Aware of innovations
_late protect policies; in rm people of rights	Well informed of personal rights; attitude of having been victimized and now en- titled to unearned benefits. Government offered itself as paternalistic; to the extent development communication is successful; people take the role of clients.
_de into existing hierar- _ with radio, TV, and _onal linking individuals _e government	Learned dependency; partici- pation consists of accepting things offered as owed, and of "complaining" (i.e., "in- forming the government that it is not doing its job well enough.")

pendency, in which "participation" consists of accepting the government's gifts as "owed" and complaining that the government is failing in specific ways to do its job well enough.

The government intended to replace fatalism and feudalism with modernity at the individual level and democratic socialism at the social level. In fact, however, the development efforts have produced a kind of neofatalism and neofeudalism, in which the people have become individualistic in their desires but remain dependent on the social structure for the fulfillment of those desires. They have learned to distrust the local social structure, but instead of developing autonomous initiative, have transferred their dependency to the central government.

THE ENGAGEMENT OF SELF IN THE DEVELOPMENT INTERACTION

Both administrative and contact agents perceive themselves as not efficacious, and this has undermined their administrative capability. Our analysis indicates that their interactions with masses and with other parts of the bureaucracy produce a specific kind of confusion. Both administrators and contact agents are caught in dilemmas; they are obliged to act effectively but all available forms of action are defined as ineffective.

Dilemmas such as these are not unique to development; they have been studied in a wide array of situations. Watzlawick, Beavin, and Jackson's (1967) research shows that when these dilemmas are salient, they are very distressing, sometimes leading to extreme forms of behavior. Another study found dilemmas of this type in situations where violence occurred between family members. Caught in the dilemma of having to act effectively, but having no effective acts available to them,

> Some try to escape . . . by creating an alternative private and unfalsifiable reality. This rarely works because we label them schizophrenics. Others try by responding passively and withdrawing into self blame. We label them depressed. Many physically internalize the problematic nature of their own cultural logic. They get ulcerative colitus. Our subjects . . . illustrate another escape tactic: lashing outward. . . .

They are, of course, "bad," even "criminal" (Harris et al. 1984, 16).

The change agents we studied were perhaps less flamboyant—or had better self-control—than the subjects described above. They have continued to serve the government and the public, but with deep discontent and concern.

THE DEPENDENCY DILEMMA

The perception that development programs have produced "learned dependency" fits poorly with the national objective for development. In fact, it puts the change agents into the dilemma summarized in Figure 6.7. Democratic socialism is a commitment obligating both of two mutually exclusive forms of action: providing for the masses' material welfare and eliciting active participation from the masses. The dilemma is created when the acts necessary to provide something—e.g., healthy drinking water—are themselves seen as increasing passivity and producing learned dependency. Change agents both must provide tap water and must not increase the masses' dependency.

THE DISTRUST DILEMMA

Contact agents are caught in an additional dilemma, as shown in Figure 6.8. The dilemma is formed by the combination of the perception of self as having limited authority and of the masses as demanding more than the agents can provide. Their choices are limited to either responding or not responding to specific demands, but either act sets into motion a sequence that makes the masses distrust them. Whether they act or do not act, the effects are equivalently distressing. No matter what they do, they disqualify themselves for a role that is essential for development.

National Goal of Democratic Socialism

Government commitment to pro-vide for the masses' material welfare	AND	Government commitment to instigate active participation by the masses
Masses show passive participation	⊃	Give them what they demand and need	OR	Withhold resources unless they display active partici-pation

IF they "give," this leads to increased dependency which pre-cludes instigating active participation.

IF they "withhold," this leads to increased discontent and blocks development programs, failing to provide for the material needs of the masses.

Figure 6.7. The dependency dilemma.

Limited Resources and Authority

| Masses demand more than change agents can give | ⊃ | Respond to a specific demand | OR | not respond to a specific demand |

IF "respond," those who made other demands will blame as being partisan, and distrust them

IF "do not respond," those who made the demand will see other responses as partisan, or will see the change agents as corrupt.

Figure 6.8. The distrust dilemma.

SEVEN

The Social Reality of the Masses

THIS CHAPTER PRESENTS our interpretation of the social reality of the masses. For the purposes of this analysis, we treat large numbers of people as if they comprise a single agent. Since no two persons are identical, this procedure risks masking idiosyncracies in order to depict commonalities within classes of people. We used this procedure without comment in our analysis of the social realities of "planners" and "change agents," but the sheer number of people involved makes the risk of untenable distortion seem greatest when referring to the "masses" as an agent in the development interaction.

There are some reasons for thinking that this is not necessarily an indefensible procedure. The people in the villages tend to think of themselves as "the masses," at least as far as development is concerned. And there are some who argue that the various traditional peoples are more alike than not, particularly in the characteristics with which we deal.

Our interpretation is based on field data from two communities. The technical details of the study, including a copy of the interview protocol and a more complete description of the data, are presented by Narula (1984). The village of Lampur, Alipur Block, Delhi, provided the rural data; and the rurban data came from the urban slum resettlement colony of Jhangirpuri in Delhi Union territory. The term "rurban" is used here, as indicated earlier, in its increasingly common meaning of a community at the periphery of urban and rural areas, inhabited primarily by rural migrants.

Lampur is designated by the government as a "progressive village." It is located about 22 kilometers from the Delhi metropolitan city, about 2 kilometers from the highway. There are about 1,500 residents in 306 households. Of the families, 221 engage in agricultural work. A primary, coeducational, one-teacher school is in the village. A women's charcha-mandal (organized discussion group) with forty members meets regularly once a month and sometimes more often. There is a cooperative society in the village but no organized discussion group for men. There is no bank or medical dispensary in the village; for these services, residents travel about 1.5 kilometers to Narela town.

The approach road and all roads in the village are metallic. Except for about twenty to thirty mud houses, all houses are made of bricks and cement. The village is fully electrified but with no street lights outside the village. Open drains exist both in and outside the village, but there is no free flow of water in the drains. There are no latrines either in the village or outside it. The use of open space outside the village for human refuse is a specific source of discontent. The lack of privacy, fear of going out of the village unaccompanied after dark, and the risk to health; all are cited as problems about which the villagers would like the government to do something. The water supply comes from handpumps, some communal and some in private houses. All give brackish water. The stagnant pond outside the village, described in chapter 1, is another source of discontent.

A total of 1,003 acres of land are cultivated. The government has two tractors available for loan to small and marginal farmers. There are eleven tractors owned by residents of the village.

The residents represent six mohallas. The predominant caste is saini; the lowest caste are the harijans, whose houses number about thirty. The other main castes are gaderia and chamars. Muslims have their own mohalla.

Some of the villagers are quite prosperous, possessing luxuries: television sets, refrigerators, washing machines, room coolers, radios, cassette recorders, ceiling fans, well furnished houses. These prosperous persons are mostly farm owners, who have tractors and other agricultural machinery.

The less prosperous residents are mostly agricultural laborers, marginal farmers, and poorly paid service workers in government offices in Delhi and nearby towns. Many of the poorer people and women are underemployed.

The pradhan (voluntary headman) is elected by the villagers and represents them in all official meetings. The current pradhan belongs to the harijan caste. The woman opinion leader, also voluntary and unpaid, is elected by the village women and is the head of the charcha mandal. The current leader belongs to the saini caste. Most villagers feel that both leaders promote the interests of their own castes.

Most of the younger generation have a high school education, although most of those over forty are illiterate.

Participation and adoption rates for Lampur are, comparatively, quite good. The masses are aware of the benefits of development. Those who commute to Delhi bring back ideas and news of higher standards of living. Some of the younger married women are from Delhi and bring with them urban influences such as women's education, personal rights, opportunities for gainful employment, luxury goods, privacy inside the home, and government provision of basic amenities such as drinking water delivered to the homes.

Compared to some other villages, Lampur women enjoy good status. There is no inhibition of education for girls, and women are quite aggressive in demanding their rights in the village and from the government.

Jhangirpuri is one of thirty-four resettlement colonies in Delhi. These conurbation colonies are planned satellites surrounding the metropolitan city.

An estimated 85,000 to 100,000 people a year migrate from the rural areas to Delhi. These migrants seek subsistence rather than self-actualization: their felt needs are for employment and survival rather than quality of life. They tend to create squatter settlements in temporary housing near their workplaces, where they suffer from inadequate services. These settlements become communities because they are composed of persons sharing a language, region, caste, and kin.

In 1975, the residents of these squatter communities began to be moved to government resettlement colonies, which were designed to provide them better socioeconomic facilities and improved quality of life. Jhangirpuri was established in 1976, located on G. T. Karnal Road between Shah Alam Bund and Bhulswa Jhangir. The total population is about 100,000 people. The area is divided into eleven housing blocks, with each block organized into plots and each plot into lanes. There are ten houses in each lane. Community latrines are provided for each lane. There are community handpumps and public water hydrants.

The general education level is primary school, with a few having a high school education. The colony was intended for poor and low-income residents, but a few upper-middle-class persons have moved in as well. The colony is economically poor, very dirty, and unkept. Participation and adoption rates for development programs is relatively good. Petty crimes are prevalent, and the residents perceive the police to be of little help. They think that they lack the amenities they are supposed to receive because they are too poor to bribe the administrative personnel who are supposed to provide them.

Electricity is provided, there are open drains for water and sullage disposal, and a public bus service provides transportation to Delhi and surrounding areas. A factory that makes frames for spectacles is located in the colony and hires residents. There is an adult literacy center and a primary school. Two allopathic and one homeopathic medical dispensaries are provided. Regular insecticide spraying is done for malarial mosquitoes, and innoculation drives are regularly held. There is a post office, bank, superbazaar, social welfare center, and police post.

Most of the residents go to nearby urban areas for employment. Many are petty traders or in low-paid jobs in government offices. A considerable number are man-riksha pullers. Women also go out of the colony for work, mostly as part time domestic help. About 25% of the colony works within the colony itself as petty traders or construction workers, and in the factory, cinema house, electric station, medical dispensaries, schools, and the Delhi Development Authority office.

COMMUNICATION MEDIA INFRASTRUCTURE

In Lampur, the male pradhan houses the community television set and is supposed to switch it on daily. About 90% of the villagers own transistor radios. Very rarely, the government field publiciity van comes to the village to screen documentaries and feature films. The nearest cinema house is about 5 kilometers away in Kundini town. Men frequently go to this cinema house, or ones in Delhi; women attend cinemas much less frequently. Villagers have frequent contact with daily newspapers and periodicals brought from Delhi. The village is frequently visited by personnel from the block development office or by various development program specialists to discuss innovations and to hear the people's complaints.

In Jhangirpuri, each block has a community center in which a television set is provided for the public. There is a cinema house in the colony, and sometimes a field publicity van comes to the colony to screen documentaries and feature films. There are few privately owned radios, but newspapers are brought from Delhi when the people go there for work. There are no development agents from any agencies providing interpersonal contact with the residents; the only contact point for the dwellers is the Delhi Development Authority office in the colony itself.

ADMINISTRATIVE INFRASTRUCTURE

In the Delhi region that includes Lampur, there is a single-tier panchyat system. The "block" is the basic unit of implementation of development programs, with the Director of Panchyat as an additional development commissioner. The subdivisional magistrate of the area is the deputy director of the panchyat. The block development officer is the head of the panchyat samiti, and is responsible for the general supervision of the village panchyat and for implementing development programs in the block. The block extension staff consists of the panchyat inspectors for various development programs, the panchyat secretaries, and the village-level workers.

Village-level workers are assigned two or three villages depending on the size of the villages, and the panchyat secretaries are assigned three or four villages according to the work load produced by the villages. The village pradhan is a member of the panchyat samiti and is the elected leader of the villagers, heading his local panchyat.

The administration of Jhangirpuri and the other resettlement colonies is handled by the Delhi Development Authority. Various development programs directed toward the community, such as family planning and health, are implemented by the centralized development agencies. Unlike the village, in which there are multiple lines of communication between the masses and development functionaries, the public officials of specific agencies are the only personal communication link between the masses and development authorities. They have neither the block structure nor indigenous opinion leadership.

Indian development analysts have always felt that a strong village opinion leadership structure was necessary for development communication and for encouraging active participation. In this study, opinion leaders were an important communication link in Lampur but not Jhangirpuri. In the rurban community, there simply was no strong opinion leadership; in the village, the people blamed the opinion leaders for failing to discharge their responsibilities in development. They accused the opinion leaders of being corrupt, of failing to convey the masses' demands effectively to the higher authorities, and of serving vested interests in the dissemination of information and the redress of grievances. Further, they blame the opinion leaders for not organizing them for self-reliant participation in development activities.

In both communities, the masses show they are aware of development efforts and interested in improving their material welfare, but not very active in giving feedback through the development bureaucracy. The amount of feedback is incommensurate with the level of involvement with development, perhaps because the pattern of interaction with contact agents is counterproductive. Through some means, the contact agents have expressed to the masses their disapproval of the form and content of the feedback they have given. When the contact agents are unreceptive, people cease offering feedback and terminate contact with the contact agent, both of which responses are inimical to active participation.

DEVELOPMENT COMMUNICATION PATTERNS

The development communication literature includes quite a lot of speculation and some data about the patterns of communication by which people learn about innovations, evaluate them, and give feedback about them to the development functionaries. Narula (1984) mapped the patterns of communication in Lampur and Jhangirpuri, differentiating between males and females. As shown in Figures 7.1 through 7.4, communication patterns were affected by the channel used, gender of participants, and type of community. Interpersonal and mass media channels were differently utilized by men and women in patterns that varied between rural and rurban areas.

Some generalizations can be discerned from the data. First, the most frequent and in many ways most important pattern of communication is horizontal among the masses. Second, interpersonal channels of top-down communication are more important than mass media for most purposes. Third, horizontal interpersonal channels among the masses are the most frequently utilized but are limited in effectiveness because they contain relatively little information, authority, and specific solutions for problems. Fourth, there are important differences between the two communities in terms of their existing communication patterns and the most effective way of communicating with people. In the village, impersonal interpersonal communication channels, as well as oral communication, play a significant role in development awareness, information, and feedback and in sensitizing the government about the masses' needs and demands. In the rurban community, these impersonal interpersonal channels were not effective.

There are different patterns of utilization for particular channels of communication, implying the need for different development communication strategies for different communities. Media channels are (not surprisingly) utilized in a one-way manner, while interpersonal channels are often two-way. Information flows through different channels than are used for discussions of information already attained. Development feedback is conveyed through different channels than attempts to sensitize development functionaries about the masses' needs and desires.

Both mass media and interpersonal channels of communication have been important in fostering development, but they have served different functions. The mass media have been effective in their first role of "information giving." In their second role—that of clarifying information and providing solutions for possible ways of action for development problems—they have not been effective either in rurban or rural communities. Since the government has invested substantial amounts of money for mass media infrastructure, the question arises about why it has failed in this second function.

Interpersonal communication channels have been those primarily responsible for creating development awareness, motivation, and participation. They are also available and primarily used for clarification of information, solutions, and possible ways of action.

Among the various mass media, only radio has effectively penetrated the mass audience. It has effectively generated development awareness both among rural and rurban communities, and has high credibility among the people. Wall posters have been effective in generating information in the rurban community, although seldom utilized in the village.

The interpersonal communication patterns contain three structures: a top-down vertical structure from government personnel to the people, a horizontal circular structure among the people, a bottom-up vertical structure from people to government. The top-down vertical structure has been helpful in creating development awareness but not high motivation for development. The horizontal circular structure created a need for development by making people articulate their demands among themselves, becoming discontent with what they have and aspir-

Communication Links

(1) Family
(2) Friends
(3) Radio
(4) Change Agents
(5) Male Opinion Leaders
(6) Visiting Program Specialists
(7) Female Opinion Leaders

(8) Television
(9) Print
(10) Drumbeaters
(11) Wall Posters
(12) Municipal Representatives
(13) Political Leaders
(14) Social Workers

Components of Development

Development Discussion
Development Information
Development Feedback by People/Government

Criterion Level for Inclusion

Minimum 40% for communication links for development information
Minimum 25% for communication links for feedback

Significance Level

———— Depicts development information sources
------ Depicts development feedback sources

 Weak communication link for development information

 Strong communication link for development information

 Strong communication link for development feedback

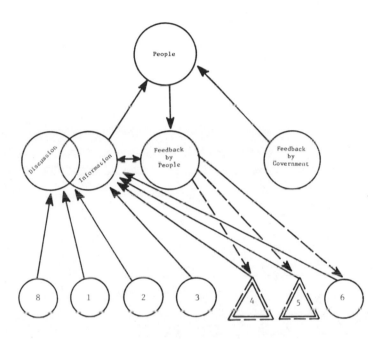

Figure 7.1. Communication links: rural males. Among rural males the most important communication links for development information discussion are family, friends, radio, change agents, opinion leaders, and visiting program specialists. The development feedback links are change agents, opinion leaders, and visiting program specialists. Change agents and opinion leaders are strong communication links both for development information and for development feedback.

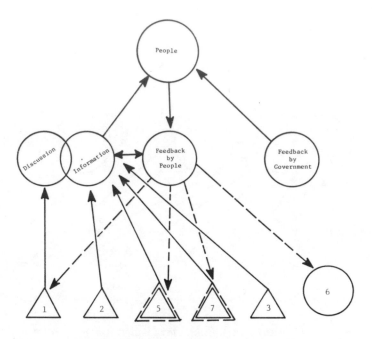

Figure 7.2. Communication links: rural females. Among rural females the important communication links for development information/discussion are family, friends, opinion leaders, and program specialists. Opinion leaders (male and female) are strong communication links both for development information and for development feedback.

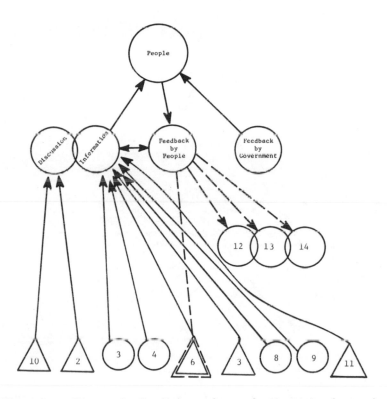

Figure 7.3. Communication links: rurban males. Among rurban males the important communication links for development information/discussion are family, friends, colleagues, radio, television, print, posters, visiting program specialists, and drumbeaters. Friends, radio, posters, and drumbeaters are the strong communication links. The development feedback links are visiting program specialists, municipal representatives, political leaders, and social workers of voluntary organizations. Visiting program specialists are the only strong feedback link.

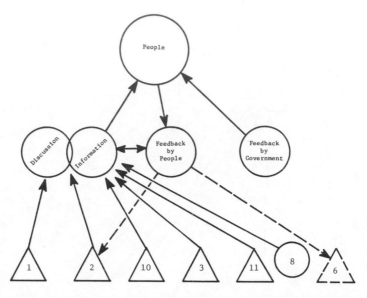

*Figure 7.4. Communication links: rurban females. Among rurban fe-
males the important links for communication of development informa-
tion/discussion are family, friends, drumbeaters, radio, television, and
posters. All are strong links except television. The development feedback
links are friends and program specialists. Program specialists are the
only strong feedback link.*

ing to a more prosperous lifestyle. The bottom-up structure is
the weakest, as a part of the passive participation of the people.

Despite the official emphasis on top-down and bottom-up patterns of communication, the most frequent communication patterns for both rural and rurban people are bottom-bottom. The
most commonly used channels are personal, with friends and
family. The largest difference in this pattern is that women con-
verse more with members of their family and less with friends
than do men.

Mass media are heavily relied upon for top-down communication. The data show that they have functioned primarily to
provide information for the people. Radio is the most frequently
cited source of development information and has high credibility. In Lampur, 83% of the men and 82% of the women cited
the radio as a medium they used; in Jhangirpuri, the statistics
were 93% of the men and 82% of the women. This finding
perhaps reflects the extensive government effort to make this a
widely used medium. The second most frequently cited medium
in Jhangirpuri was that of wallposters, with 96% of the men and
72% of the women designating it as a useful medium.

The mass media are not cited by the residents of either community as important means of clarifying information, providing
solutions, or suggesting possible ways of acting, although these
are explicit functions assigned to the media by the planners.

In top-down communication through interpersonal channels,
some important differences between communities, between
castes, and between the sexes occur. In Lampur, men get information about development projects from the male opinion
leader (67%); 76% of the women get information from both
male and female opinion leaders, and 60% from their families.
Higher-caste men, however, get information from government
officials and program specialists more than lower-caste men. In
Jhangirpuri, both men and women get information from
friends (males, 76%; females, 86%) and drumbeaters (males,
55%; females, 62%), who announce development activities in the
residential complex itself. Men (67%) more than women (38%)
cite program specialists as a source of information.

Two-way communication is achieved when the masses give

feedback to the government—feedback that is heard and acted upon—and the results communicated back to the masses. This laudable process does not often occur. The process is blocked in its earliest stage; the people do not give very much feedback, and when they do, it is primarily in the form of demands that the government do something for them rather than suggesting solutions to problems. The reason for this pattern is not hard to find. The residents of Jhangirpuri describe themselves as having no contact with opinion leaders (males, 77%; females, 82%) or change agents (males, 93%; females, 92%), and the residents of Lampur perceive the opinion leaders (males, 63%; females, 66%) and the change agents (males, 72%; females, 64%) as disapproving of their even giving feedback, particularly solutions.

When there is feedback, it is usually given to the information source. This creates a very different pattern in the two communities, since the rural community has many more interpersonal sources. Compared to Lampur, Jhangirpuri residents do not give very much feedback.

In summary, the masses assess their communication with contact agents and administrators as important because these persons are seen as controlling resources and having access to information, but their credibility is low because they are seen as serving vested interests and disapproving of the masses' active participation. The most frequently used and influential forms of communiction are with friends and family. These persons have high credibility but are not seen as having resources or information, and hence their evaluation in terms of potential for development is low. Certain media are heavily utilized, but this is one-way communication, limited to an information-giving function.

These data suggest that the patterns of development communication have changed over the past twenty years—perhaps as a function of development efforts themselves. Figure 7.5 is a composite model of development communication patterns based on research studies conducted during the 1960s and 1970s. This model stresses the central role of a strong local leadership who express development demands and impose sanc-

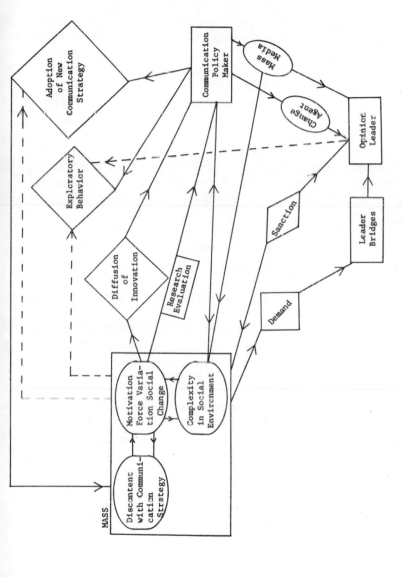

Figure 7.5. Development communication model based on research conducted in the 1960s and 1970s. Broken lines imply lack of effort.

tions. The data from Lampur and Jhangirpuri, shown in Figure 7.6, suggest a significantly different pattern.

First, the data in Figure 7.6 indicate more participation by the masses and more interaction with officials and less with opinion leaders. For example, they are more likely to make their demand directly to officials, not through opinion leaders. They no longer care about the sanctions imposed by the opinion leaders.

Second, research conducted during the 1960s and 1970s showed that the masses' discontent was focused on the communication strategies of the government. The masses perceived the government's development planning as irrelevant to them, and the communication strategies were designed to make them aware of development needs. At the present time, the masses are much more aware of development needs and projects, and are discontented because their demands have not been met. They have moved from a belief that the government has no concern for or interest in their economic and social condition to a perception of the government as a failed provider of goods and services.

Third, the present data indicate that the masses are much more knowledgeable about the development bureaucracy than they used to be. Specifically, they seem to have a much improved notion of which channels of communication ought to be useful to them.

Fourth, in the 1960s and 1970s, the processes of development communication made the social environment of the villages more complex than they were. They were deeply enmeshed in traditional social patterns, and resistent to change and modernization. At present, increased complexity is not a function of development communication.

Fifth, in the older pattern, development took place through innovation. The masses had to be made aware that a condition with which they were very familiar was a problem that could and should be solved; they had to be informed of a new practice that was a solution and urged to accept it. Now, the masses are aware of the problems and the practices; development is a matter of diffusion, of getting the masses to adopt strategies with which they are already familiar.

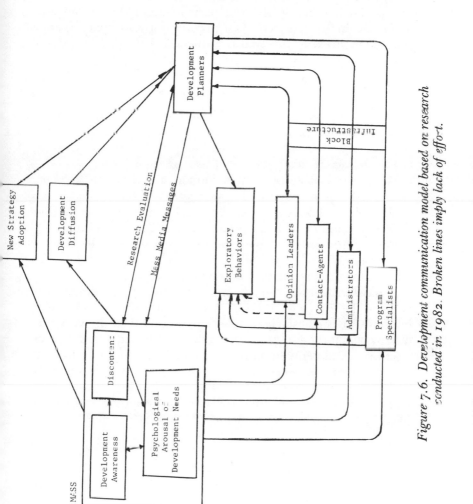

Figure 7.6. Development communication model based on research conducted in 1982. Broken lines imply lack of effort.

There is another point of comparison, in which the two models of development communication do not differ. The masses do not display high levels of active participation either in our data or in the earlier research. The prevailing passive participation is a major threat to the goal of achieving self-sustaining development.

PASSIVE PARTICIPATION

The masses were expected to become active participants in the process of development. The planners thought that specific factors obstructed development, including the fatalistic philosophy of life characteristic of Indian village society, a strong allegiance to the local social structure that contained exploitative linkages, and lack of awareness of the alternatives. They thought they could remove those obstacles by a combination of direct action, legislation, and development communication—including information, education, and communication (IEC) for the masses. With these obstacles out of the way, the masses would readily move into an active participation in development.

It has not worked out as expected, and—surprisingly—not because the efforts of the government have been unsuccessful in removing the obstacles to participation. Rather, the very process by which these obstacles have been removed has produced another and potentially more serious impediment to participatory development: learned dependency. The development communication objectives of awareness, involvement, and discontent—thought to be the sufficient prerequisites of active participation—have been achieved, but active participation has not.

In Lampur, 74% of the men were "highly aware" of development programs operating in their region, and 62% of the women had at least "medium awareness." In Jhangirpuri, 89% of the men and 78% of the women reported "high awareness." Involvement was measured by participation in communication about development programs. About a third of the residents of both communities of both sexes reported talking about development projects "almost daily" and two-thirds or more were involved in development discussions "occasionally." Less than 7% of any group reported "rarely" engaging in these discussions. A majority of both samples expressed at least "medium discontent" with the success of development programs in meeting their needs (rural males 59%, females 60%; rurban males 62%; females 78%) and approval of development programs (in Lampur, 94% of the men and 78% of the women approved the agricultural program and 98% of the men and 100% of the women approved public family planning projects; in Jhangirpuri, 84% of the men and 64% of the women approved public transit programs and 86% of the men and 84% of the women approved health care).

However, the amount of actual participation in development programs—as differentiated from talking about them or expressing discontent with existing conditions—is not very high. In the rural sample, 49% of the men evidenced a "medium level" of activity and 60% of the women a "low level" of activity. In the rurban sample, no more than a "medium level" of activity was engaged in by 54% of the men and 66% of the women.

Further, this participation is virtually exclusively limited to passive forms. In Lampur, 23% of the men and 22% of the women expressed a willingness to make demands on the government by protesting and representing their group. In Jhangirpuri, the figures were 61% for men and 60% for women. However, only 13% of the men and 4% of the women in Jhangirpuri, and none of the men or women in Lampur, even *said* they would participate in organized efforts to accomplish development objectives. These findings suggest a pattern of passive participation, lack of initiative, and dependency upon the group for participation. This pattern is stronger for the rural than the rurban group.

One unanticipated obstacle to active participation is the masses' lack of faith in the contact agents as means of communication about development. Another is the lack of cooperation among the people in conducting development activites. In the village, the noncooperation is attributable to casteism and the disparity between the haves and the have-nots. In the rurban community, it is accounted for by regionalism and the noncohesiveness of the community. In both cases, however, the communities do not look to themselves for meaningful solutions of their needs. Instead, they make development demands on the government. The most significant contribution the people have made toward development is their attitude of discontent. This attitude leads to psychological arousal and awareness of needs. But the research results show that the conventional wisdom, which holds that people are activated to participate when there is development awareness and discontent, is not true.

The difference in the developmental infrastructure was apparent when respondents were asked to describe the type of activity they would envision as effective means of getting the government to be responsive. The rural sample cited ways of going "through the proper channels" by petitioning the government, working through change agents, and the like. In one way, this betokens a confidence in the social institutions; but in another, it reflects an acquired passive orientation of telling someone else to do what needs being done. In Jhangirpuri, where there are few if any interpersonal channels to convey information bottom-up, 70% of the men and 52% of the women would organize informal groups; peaceful demonstrations to register their development needs and demands were endorsed by 62% of the men and 68% of the women. In Jhangirpuri, the use of media forums, opinion leaders, and change agents was not contemplated because these do not exist in that rurban community. About a third of the women in both groups and about 20% of the men would do nothing, feeling they had no efficacious recourse.

When asked why they were not willing to engage in active participation, a variety of reasons were cited. A relatively large minority of respondents expressed a feeling of inefficacy in self-development and self-reliance, both as individuals (rural men 31%, women 48%; rurban men 11%, women 28%) and as a part of their community (rural men 37%, women 34%; rurban men 6%, women 28%). A large majority perceived government functionaries as ineffective, and the analysis of data shows a high relation between these perceptions and forms of participation. Particularly in the rurban sample, the people feel that development functionaries are indifferent to their grievances (men 98%, women 100%). A majority of respondents believe that contact agents block the flow of information (rural men 63%, women 74%; rurban men 98%, women 96%), and that administrators are indifferent to their demands (rural men 74%; women 34%; rurban men 96%, women 86%).

How Development Works

The masses' participation in development is guided by their concept of the purpose and process of development, including their part in it. From the masses' perspective, the sequence of events in the development interaction begins with government activity. They do not share the planners' vision of development in the context of British colonialism and international relationships, nor the change agents' conception of a partnership between government and people for mutual benefit. Rather, they see development as something initiated by the government.

At the beginning of the development period, the government engaged in three types of acts: legislation to break up vested interests in the local communities, direct actions to provide necessary infrastructure for development programs, plan publicity announcing the government's intention to better the standard of life for the people. Government officials thought of only the latter as a form of communication, the other two as not. From the vantage of the people, however, all three forms of action had "message value." If anything, the first two spoke more loudly than the third. Roads, the redistribution of land, the establishment of the Block Development administrative hierarchy, and so forth, were no less ways of creating and managing social reality simply because the government did not intend them to be or perceive them as "messages."

The masses felt themselves strongly "communicated with," and interpreted the government as nominating itself for the role of perpetual provider of the benefits and resources of modernity. Later, they "heard" the government declare itself as uninterested in their (the masses') suggestions or initiatives in development programs. And still later, they found the government showing itself as ineffective and inefficient in the delivery of the benefits and resources of development.

Programs of direct action seem most directly to show the government as the willing and voluntary provider of goods and services. This combined with three other aspects of the interaction between the masses and the government to complete a perception of the government as a surrogate parent—at least as far as development goes.

First, the masses felt that their suggestions and contributions to the development effort were unwanted and unappreciated. The criticisms of the Panchyat Raj, regardless of their merits from an administrative viewpoint, constituted a rejection of the masses' contribution to development. The rural elite, who had resources that could be contributed to development programs, were frequently told they should not prosper disproportionately from development, so withheld their resources to keep themselves from contributing disproportionately to it. As a result, the elite used the poor sections as models for participation, but these people are predominantly in a survival mode, more inclined to act in terms of immediate needs than a comprehensive development program. In particular, the idea of donating what scarce resources they had in hopes of an eventual community benefit is hard for the very poor to grasp. Development functionaries often reported that the suggestions made by the masses were unrealistic and unworkable, and perhaps they were. But from a communication perspective, what was communicated to the masses by what they perceived as the government's inattention to and dismissal of their suggestions was a further negotiation of a parental relationship in which independent, self-initiated action was inappropriate.

Second, the legislation designed to break exploitative linkages had the effect of transferring the traditional villagers' dependency on the local social structure to the national government. It did not achieve its goal of producing self-reliant, individualist persons, although the dependency on the national government disrupted traditional leadership structures. The result looked like individualistic dependency on an absentee parent—and a not very effective parent at that.

Traditional Indian village society is characterized by individual dependency within relatively autonomous social structures. The government efforts to reduce the economic effects of the caste system, to put into place an elaborate, labor-intensive hierarchy of block functionaries, and to disrupt (e.g., with the Land Ceiling Act) tradititional forms of status and power had the effect of intruding the national government into the local community. Among other things, this made it impossible for the masses to perceive local social institutions as autonomous. Given these undeniable intrusions, the people could respond in either of two ways. They could develop a radically novel sense of individual autonomy, like that envisioned in the stereotype of "modern man." Or they could shift their sense of dependency from the local to the national government, forming in their social reality at least something of a "national village." The latter is the more likely response under any circumstances, and particularly when the government was in other ways strongly nominating itself for the role of provider and caretaker. The people continued to perceive themselves as personally ineffective in achieving development objectives, and looked elsewhere—a little farther from home than before—for help.

If the goal of development is to make individuals more "modern," then an individual's perception of self as "one of the masses" is itself a problem. Among other things, this concept of self lacks what Pareek (1968) called "extension motive": a sense of self-efficacy in changing the environment or one's manner of life.

Finally, the masses began to perceive the government as ineffective and inefficient in the delivery of the benefits and resources of development. The implications of this perception derive from the relationship between themselves and the government. But their concept of this relationship is quite different from the government's own view. The government sees itself as having limited resources to meet a virtually infinite demand across the whole country; but the masses see the government as having virtually infinite resources with which to meet their own specific, local needs. The masses' perspective is focused on their own community needs, and they are repeatedly

confronted by the frustration of particular problems going un-
met no matter how many times they complain and bring their
needs to the attention of the governmental "parent." Rather
than seeing the government as a willing but limited partner in
development, they see the government as a bad parent who does
not successfully discharge its responsibilities.

This interpretive account shows the absence of "active participation" by the masses as a communicative act, not simply as a
"trait" like stubborness or laziness. The masses see their behavior toward the government and development as being quite appropriate. If the government has nominated itself as exercising
parental responsibility, then the masses have done all they
should when they articulate their felt needs, demand immediate
implementation of development projects, and insist on immediate redress for their grievances. If they were to explore and
suggest solutions to these problems, or offer to contribute
money or labor for the programs designed for them, this would
be a grossly inappropriate behavior toward a parent.

When the government persists in acting like a bad parent, the
masses can "help" by becoming quite energetic in drawing the
failures of the government to its attention. The masses protest
what they see as government failures verbally, by strikes, by violent agitation, by grafitti, by gherao (locking administrators in
their offices), and by repeated petitions to concerned authorities.
It is hard for the contact agents to see these forms of actions as
supportive of the development movement, but within the
masses' social reality, they are. They are ways of exhorting the
government to play well the part it took for itself.

This aspect of the interaction between the masses and the
government is particularly unfortunate. At least as we construe
it, each agent urges the other to intensify efforts but interprets
those efforts when intensified as being less desirable than before.
This is a pattern Watzlawick, Beavin, and Jackson (1967) call
"symmetrical escalation," in which each successive attempt in
good faith to accommodate to the other agent exacerbates the
misunderstanding and the failure to achieve a coordinated management of meaning.

Our characterization of the masses' perception of the government is based on the data, but they did not supply the "parent" metaphor. We think it is a defensible interpretation. Human actions always refer beyond themselves, and that to which they refer is almost always—and often primarily—a matter of relationships. Watzlawick, Beavin, and Jackson (1967) took as axiomatic that persons always communicate at two levels, one of "content" and the other of "relationship." Bateson (1972, 470) attributed the primacy of relational considerations to the fact that humans are mammals.

> Mammals in general, and we among them, care extremely, not about episodes, but about the patterns of their relationships. When you open the refrigerator door and the cat comes up and makes a certain sound, she is not talking about liver or milk, though you may know very well that that is what she wants. You may be able to guess correctly and give her that—if there is any in the refrigerator. What she actually says is something about the relationship between herself and you. If you translated her message into words, it would be something like, "dependency, dependency, dependency." She is talking, in fact, about a rather abstract pattern within a relationship. From that assertion of a pattern, you are expected to go from the general to the specific—to deduce "milk" or "liver."
> This is crucial. This is what mammals are about. They are concerned with patterns of relationship, with where they stand in love, hate, respect, dependency, trust, and similar abstractions vis-a-vis somebody else.

The rules of parenting in Indian family life seem very close to some of the patterns we observed in the data. If so, the concept of development by the masses is like that of family life, in which the parents are to be responsible providers and the children are obliged to tell the parents what they need and to point out instances in which the parents inadequately fill their roles.

An Ethic of Proportional Effort

The masses seem to have developed what we call an "ethic of proportional effort." This ethic holds that there is something wrong, perhaps even shameful, in exerting a *disproportionate ef-*

fort to accomplish a task that will have *equivalent benefits* for the whole group. This ethic seemed to be the context for the phrase often encountered when one asks the masses why they do not engage in various forms of active participation. "Why should *I*?" they ask, with the emphasis on the personal pronoun. When additional talk is elicited, they frequently refer to others who would benefit from their activity but who are not contributing proportional effort. The hypothesis of an ethic of proportional effort in the social reality of the masses is significant, if true, because such an ethic is the antithesis of the ethic implied in the concept of democratic socialism.

This is a robust social reality, which withstands disappointment. The masses, having accepted the government's offer to assume responsibility for their lives, asked for additional benefits. In most cases, these requests were not met, in part because the government has limited resources and in part because the administrators did not want to inculcate precisely this kind of dependency. For whatever reason, the government's failure to deliver development commodities has not been taken as a sufficient reason for the masses to reconceptualize the relationship with the government or to reduce their dependency on the government. Rather, the government's failure has led to more energetic and insistent demands that the government play its role better. These take the form of increased demands for development benefits and criticism of the government.

This social reality can be expressed as four "action rules" that occur under the context of the parental relationship with the government. First, the masses feel that it is obligatory for them to obey the government's directives, including the directive to allow it to assume parental responsibility for development.

Second, the masses feel prohibited from taking initiatives in development projects; this would show disrespect and a lack of confidence in the parent who requested responsibility.

Third, the masses feel that it is permissible, perhaps obligatory, to complain about the government's failures to fulfill their promises to provide for their material needs and satisfactions.

Fourth, the masses feel prohibited from exerting disproportional effort for projects that will benefit other people equally. To do so makes one seem foolish, exploited by others; an elitist, flaunting one's superiority; or ambitious, trying to gain social power.

EIGHT

The Interaction among Development Agents

IN CHAPTERS 5, 6, and 7, we described development as it is experienced by the major agents involved: planners, contact agents, and masses. That analysis showed that development means very different things to each group. Further, each of the agents experiences tensions and dilemmas because of the way their perceptions of themselves, of each other, and of development itself interrelate.

In different ways, each of these agents is distressed and discontented. The dilemma confronting planners originates in the unresolved tensions in their commitment both to democracy and socialism. Change agents are caught in distrust and dependency binds, such that they must act but no act available to them is right. The masses have learned dependency in such a way that the more they do what seems appropriate, the more they are told they are failing to support development. All the agents are dissatisfied with the way development has happened, and each blames the others.

How has this happened? How can this distressing situation be explained and countered?

We are tempted to ask, Who is really to blame? Which group correctly perceives the failures of the others? Which agent should be persuaded or compelled to change so the others will be less discontented and the task of development completed?

The "communication perspective" teaches us that this way of posing questions itself is wrong. Questions focusing praise or blame on particular agents or acts are framed in a vocabulary that obscures vital parts of the process, such as the interrelations among agents, the sequences of actions, and (potentially complex and conflicted) patterns in the logic of meaning and action produced by the interaction of these agents in this particular historical setting. Any answer to questions that assume individual culpability or praise distorts what the communication perspective assumes is happening.

From that perspective, the actual sequence of acts performed by multiple agents, each of whom is seeking coherence and coordination, are central for analysis. Each act by one of the agents, in its temporal context, is interpreted by all of the agents, and these interpretations guide their subsequent acts, which are interpreted . . . and so on. This unfolding sequence is not unilaterally controlled by any agent. In fact, the "logic" of this action chain is more likely than not to deviate significantly from the intentions and expectations of any agent. Further, there is no reason to suppose that all of the agents interpret any act or the sequence of acts in the same way. It is very possible that several agents have not only differing but incommensurate perceptions of action sequences in which they participated. Moreover, we anticipate that the emerging pattern of acts will have reflexive effects on the social realities of the agents involved. Particularly if they perceive the sequence of actions as deviating from what they expected, agents are likely to revise their own concepts of self, of other agents, or of what they are doing. Finally, all of this is more likely to occur to the extent that agents are more deeply enmeshed in the interaction.

Does the communication perspective provide a way of understanding development in India more adequately than the search for someone or some policy to blame? We think so, and we think the answer lies in the particular, historical sequence of events in the interaction among planners, change agents, and the masses.

The problem is not—or at least was not initially—one of will or motivation. Our data suggest that the various agents as a whole have set high goals and pursued them tenaciously. Tragically, these goals have not always been fully commensurate with those of other agents, or clearly expressed. Repeated frustration more often *produced* rather than *resulted from* apathy, laziness, and discouragement. Ironically, sincerity or a high degree of enmeshment with developmental goals and activities is part of the problem. The most well-intentioned efforts to accommodate and coordinate with other agents have sometimes appeared to those others as recalcitrant obstruction. Attempts to "improve" the interaction have sometimes consisted of doing more of the same thing, which only escalated the problem. Other participants have found themselves in binds in which every act available to them seemed only to make problems worse.

Further, we have no evidence to suggest that the problem lies in the personal moralities of various individuals or the lack of expertise at any given level of the development hierarchy. Specific instances of corruption or poor judgment can be found in any project involving this many people for this period of time handling such an array of resources, and no doubt outstanding examples of such regrettable instances can be cited among development personnel. When something is going badly, it is tempting to find a vivid example of wrongdoing or incompetence and blame *it* for the unsatisfying result. But this risks confusing a conspicuous symptom or irrelevant detail with the cause.

Our analysis of the social realities of various agents shows that there is a great deal of difference in their perception of particular acts. What, e.g., a contact change agent sees as "appropriate" or "the best I can do given my limited resources" may be interpreted by others as lazy, selfish, or blatantly partisan.

In our judgment, the widespread assumption of rampant corruption poses a more serious problem than actual corrupt acts. This should not be construed as tolerating actual instances of partisanship and malfeasance, but as emphasizing the importance of achieving a reciprocated perception among the masses, the development bureaucracy, and the government that the system is comprised of competent people working with good motives to achieve development objectives. Such a climate of trust is necessary if participants in the interaction are to act in good faith.

We suggest that the widespread dissatisfactions with development efforts can be attributed to inherent features of social action and to the particular history of the interaction among these agents. The combination of the dilemmas, binds, and dependency described in chapters 5, 6, and 7 create a particularly distressing—but far from unprecedented—pattern. All of the participants in the pattern are aware of it, although most describe it in a vocabulary that obscures some of its most important aspects, including the fact that it is produced and sustained by an *interaction* among agents. All of the participants are dissatisfied with it, and all—in one way or another—have tried to change it. The ironic and vicious nature of the pattern, however, is its homeostatic stability. The pattern is such that the actions taken by various agents to change it themselves become the forces that perpetuate it.

The logic of the sequence of actions has trapped the participants, each in a unique manner. To understand how this came about, it is necessary not only to understand each set of agents but to reconstruct the sequence of interactions among agents.

Figure 8.1 presents a summary of the interaction among agents, deliberately taking a vantage that includes the social realities of all agents, the actions of all agents in sequence, and the reflexive effects of that sequence on the agents themselves.

Creating Development Awareness: The First Plan

The first five-year plan initiated development projects on a national scale. It was understood by the planners as a means to create development awareness among people by informing, educating, and motivating them to accept the need for development. This was also the period in which the technologies of radio, print, film, and interpersonal and traditional channels were used as means of plan publicity. The goal of development efforts was the promotion of effective public participation. Awareness was created by an extension education approach, development of extension agencies, and development of interpersonal communication linkages.

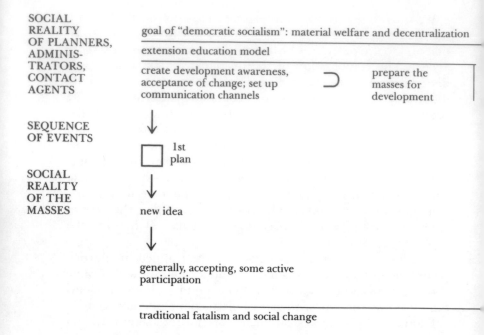

Figure 8.1. A diagram of the development interaction. This diagram depicts the "interaction" among agents in a manner more compatible with the communication perspective than is the segmented description of each agent. The diagram is to be read in a serpentine fashion: begin at the upper left, go to the lower left, take a step to the right, then upward, a step to the right, then downward, etc. Vertical movements are signaled by directional arrows, horizontal movements by the horseshoe-shaped disjunctive symbol. The solid and broken squares indicate levels of contextualization.

massive changes de-
spite development
promises;
al social structures,
bureaucracy inhibiting
development progress
	reform village structure
	and
	set up participatory
	  model;
	  1. community develop-
	      ment
	  2. Panchayat Raj
	  3. cooperatives
		remove impediments
		for development
		and
		achieve
		  1. self reliance
		  2. local administration
		  3. generate economic
		      resources

☐ 2nd plan

(elites) an attack on their social position

(poor) government giving them handouts

Figure 8.1 Continued.

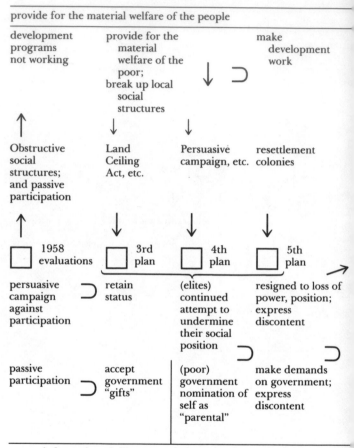

SOCIAL REALITY OF PLANNERS, ADMINISTRATORS, CONTACT AGENTS

provide for the material welfare of the people

development programs not working

provide for the material welfare of the poor; break up local social structures

make development work

SEQUENCE OF EVENTS

SOCIAL REALITY OF THE MASSES

Obstructive social structures; and passive participation

Land Ceiling Act, etc.

Persuasive campaign, etc.

resettlement colonies

1958 evaluations

3rd plan

4th plan

5th plan

persuasive campaign against participation

retain status

(elites) continued attempt to undermine their social position

resigned to loss of power, position; express discontent

passive participation

accept government "gifts"

(poor) government nomination of self as "parental"

make demands on government; express discontent

aware, informed, and discontented about development; "ethic of dispro portional effort" concern to make a partnership with the people and provide material welfare for the poor

discontent with government handling of development	redesign development plans: BMN model and participatory model	planners: "charmed loop" reinforcing centralization

⊃ (between columns 1 and 2) ⊃ (between columns 2 and 3)

administrators: "dependency bind"
contact agents: "dependency bind" and "mistrust-bind"

↑ (col 1)   ↓ (col 2)   ↑ (col 3)

□ 1978 elections	□ 6th plan	□ "learned dependency"

↓ (col 2)   ↑ (col 3)

let government take responsibility for development

be a good helpful government
be a good "parent"

government takes responsibility for providing material welfare;

government blames elites for failure of development

government asks for self-sacrificial involvement by elites

accept continued "parental" role by government

reject blame, refuse to engage in disproportionate contributions

cooperate with government

maintain self-respect

⊃ (between columns 2 and 3)   ⊃ (between columns 3 and 4)

The masses responded enthusiastically to these acts by the government. They were willing to contribute in cash, labor, and kind toward development. There was some resistance based on a perception that development was inimical to their traditional values and ways of life, but this resistence was met with patience and efforts toward gradual change in the attitudes of the people.

Changing Traditional Social Structure

Prime Minister Nehru was concerned that the government had not yet delivered on its promise to bring social and economic programs to the people. Various evaluations and recommendations by planners warned that the people were not yet ready to accept development, and urged a continuation of efforts to create attitudes conducive to development. However, Nehru was concerned that if the social and economic programs were not delivered to the masses speedily, they would become disillusioned with the government, since the government had publically promised to achieve these goals. As a result, he commissioned a sweeping new program that set up an extensive development bureaucracy and reorganized the social structure of villages throughout the country.

The new program was perceived as initiating a phased sequence of development. The first phase consisted of strong centralized programs to change the masses and then give way to decentralized development. The major obstacle envisioned was the rural elites, whose social position was seen as a barrier between the government and the socially deprived sections of the society.

The second five-year plan created the block development infrastructure and Panchyat Raj for administering community development programs in the villages through locally generated resources by means of cooperatives. The government saw their activities as giving power to the people, enabling them to develop self-reliance, exercise local administration, and utilize local resources more effectively.

The planners blamed administrators for the failure of the community development program. They thought the administrators were apathetic and inefficient, that they lacked coordination between planning and implementation, and that they were excessively target minded. They visualized the panchyat as the structured leadership through which the villages could be mobilized for development, and relied upon them to elicit local initiative and interest in economy and efficiency. In addition, the panchyat were expected to cope with the whole range of community problems related to the modernization process.

The rural elites opposed these projects. They perceived the government as asking them to participate in a program that, if effective, would take away their social position, economic power, perquisites, and traditional forms of influence on the people. They were apprehensive about the Panchyat Raj system because it gave everyone in the village an equal vote. Since there were more of the lower castes than the upper, this meant that there was at least an implicit threat to their position. Even so, they objected less to the creation of panchyat—as long as they were able to exercise leadership through these councils—than to community development and cooperatives. As long as they were leaders of the panchyat, this only changed the name but not the fact of their domination of the local community. The community development program and cooperatives, on the other hand, threatened their position directly because they were bypassed in a special relationship between the government and the weaker sections of the community.

The weaker sections of the rural communities supported these projects but did not have sufficient resources to contribute to them to make them broadly effective. The rural elites engaged in a vigorous persuasive campaign urging nonparticipation in the development programs. Among other things, they argued that these programs were contradictory to the religion and traditions of the community and were dominated by outside forces—urban Indians and foreigners.

PROGRAM EVALUATIONS

Reports of the Programme Evaluation Organization and other government appraisals were interpreted as showing that the masses are not resistent or indifferent to development but engaged only in passive participation.

From our perspective, it is likely that the masses never understood the government's perception of development as a national partnership to expunge the economic ravages of colonialism and to achieve modernization. Their social realities were such that development activities were interpreted as a government nomination of itself for a parental role of being responsible for their material welfare. For the rural elites, this intrusive self-nomination was generally threatening, appearing to rebuke them for having attained a position of relative affluence and promising to disengage them from their positions of privilege and influence. For the weaker sections of the communities, the development activities did not mesh with their social reality at all, and were more a matter of the government's willingness to give them a handout than a call to a new national program of development.

However, the planners interpreted the results as indicating that the existing programs had failed, for two reasons. First, the people were not participating in the manner in which they were expected. Development was supposed to be a people's program with government participation, but had turned out to be a government program with (an inadequate level of) people's participation. Second, the social structure of the villagers was proving more obdurate than expected. By 1958, the government acknowledged the difficulties it was having in progressively delegating the implementation and planning of development programs to the people. An often-repeated remark from this era captured the idealism and the frustration among the planners: "The people's movement is on, but the people's representatives are yet to join." Because the village leadership was opposed to the programs, they did not understand their responsibilities in the context of changing situations and values.

These results were particularly discouraging because they questioned the ability of the people to conduct development programs at all. In the late 1950s, the government assessed the effects of its programs to initiate structural changes in the villages. The results indicated that the purpose of these changes—

to facilitate participation in democractic institutions in the local communities—were not being achieved: traditional patterns of exploitation and domination were continuing. The planners had intended the panchyat to be a spokespiece for the village and an intermediary between the villagers and the government. The lower castes were to be represented in the panchyat since the election system gives every villager a vote. However, the communication pattern that actually emerged through the implementation of Panchyat Raj was very different, and created a "communication gap" and "development benefit gap" between the haves and the have-nots.

In 1952, the government decided to decentralize development by investing primary administrative responsibilities in the Panchyat Raj. In 1958, they interpreted the data from various evaluations as indicating that this had not been successful because the rural elites were obstructing development and the people were not actively participating. They decided to take what we have characterized as a parental role, in which their task was to break through the remaining vestiges of traditional social structure in order to reach and uplift the socially deprived. This purpose was expressed in the next three five year plans.

The government used a basic mimimum needs model, which is highly centralized and seeks to circumvent existing economic and social structures in order to reach the "marginals." In the five-year plan, this took the specific form of providing resettlement colonies for the urban poor who had been ignored by previous, rural-oriented programs. Additional legislation was passed in order to further weaken the power of the rural elites. For example, the Land Ceiling Act and the abolition of bonded labor and the village moneylenders deprived the rural elites of many of their sources of power.

Considerable attention was given to communication, primarily to reach those who had previously not been contacted by the government. Their analysis was that the pattern of media and interpersonal channels had produced an information glut in some progressive rural and urban communities, but that backward rural and urban areas were neglected. Also, there was an information imbalance and blockages by the elite. Finally, there was an expanded emphasis on changing attitudes and behaviors of the people. Even this attention to persuasion was an expression of the government's assuming the responsibility for making development work—even if it meant persuading the people to act in unfamiliar ways.

The rural elite perceived these programs as a continued and escalated attempt to undermine their own position, and they gave up. They became resigned to the government's development efforts. This reflects a "dependent" attitude, in which they said, in effect, "You have forcibly taken over, now do it yourself!"

The weaker sections of the rural communities saw the government as protecting them in something like a parental role. In the social vacuum caused by the disruption of the traditional patterns, they accepted the government's nomination of itself as provider of development benefits. They were happy to make demands on the government, like a child makes demands on a parent, and this was seen as the appropriate response to the government's initiative.

Both elites and the weaker sections of the rural communities were responsive to the persuasive campaign designed to change their attitudes and behavior. They became informed about development programs, discontent with the status quo, desirous of change, and had high expectations for the benefits they personally would derive from what the government was going to do.

In light of these expectations, they became discontented with the government's performance. This discontent was expressed in many ways, including messages sent through the contact agents to the administrators. However, the most telling message was the election of 1977.

"Remove Poverty"

Nehru was right: A government that fails to deliver what it has promised for many years will lose favor with the masses and, in a democracy, will be voted out of office. That is exactly what happened. A powerful message of discontent by the people was conveyed in the 1977 elections when Janata Party was elected.

This result came as a great surprise to political experts in

India, since the Janata Party was widely perceived as too weak to form an effective government. Various election research studies found that the masses did not expect the Janata Party to be effective, but since it had made "Remove Poverty" its election manifesto, they thought that a vote for this party was a way of signaling their discontent with the delivery of development promises and a statement about what they wanted as highest priority by the government.

In its brief tenure in office, the Janata Party was not noticeably more effective than the previous government in achieving development objectives. However, when the Congress (I) Party returned to office in 1980, they had clearly heard the message: The people were discontented with the way development had gone.

Indira Gandhi's government was influenced by public opinion calling for the immediate solution to poverty and by the international development community's emphasis on participatory models of development. It instituted the sixth five-year plan which included annual rolling plans with evaluation procedures.

The plan contained two basic thrusts. One is a continuation of the basic miminum needs model, the other is a participatory model. These models have contradictory implications. The basic miminum needs model is highly centralized, envisioning a strong government breaking through local social structures in order to contact and provide for marginals. The participatory model is decentralized, envisioning a strong local organization that devises and implements need-based programs within local communities.

Both aspects of this contradiction were communicated to the masses, by different agents. The planners, using mass media going directly from the central government to the people, emphasized the message of basic miminum needs. They were perceived as continuing to assume responsibility for delivering the benefits of development to the maximum number of people. The rural elite were excluded from the benefits and identified as part of the problem, and asked to stay out of the way. Our data show that the rural elite see themselves as being bypassed by development because the government shows partiality toward the weaker sections. One aspect of the rural elite's discontent stems from their desire for a special track of development programs for themselves.

The administrators and contact agents, on the other hand, used interpersonal channels to emphasize the message of participation. Unlike the planners, change agents—perhaps because they are thinking of a different "section" of the masses—do not perceive the masses as helpless. The administrators perceive them as dependent and the contact agents as demanding, but far from helpless.

The rural elite perceived change agents as blaming them for the failure of development. The message is that because they have not been sufficiently active in participating in development efforts, the benefits of development have not occurred. The elites are not willing to accept this blame. For years, they have been "told" (although perhaps unintentionally) by the planners that they are exploiting the helpless weaker groups and that their behavior makes existing community social structures dysfunctional. They have been told explicitly to stop their exploitative behavior and the central government will see to the basic mimimum needs of the very poor. This message has been reinforced by administrators who discourage or are indifferent to their participation. The administrators have told them for years that they are incompetent to design or implement development projects. However, this accusation lacks credibility because the rural elite view change agents as unfairly partial to vested interests and as obstructing lines of communication with development officials. As a result, they feel helpless to do anything.

A BLOCK RECURSIVE PATTERN

The interaction described in this chapter and summarized in Figure 8.1 can be described as "block recursive." The shape of the pattern was established early, at least during the second plan. The government's perception of the masses as passive and requiring structural changes, and the masses' perception of the government in a parental role, provided the context within which the whole sequence of the interaction was framed. Within this frame, acts designed to "improve" the situation in fact perpetuated the pattern.

It is possible to impose any number of "punctuations" on a sequence of acts, alternately defining a particular behavior as a "cause" or an "effect" and even changing the meaning of the act by seeing it in various places within a subsequence. As we interpret the interaction among development agents, much of the discontent experienced by those agents derives from a particular punctuation.

There are no "truth conditions" against which any punctuation of a sequence of events can be judged true or false. It may be extremely important that various persons punctuate their interaction differently, but this is a matter for persuasion and understanding, not for adjudication between "right" and "wrong" punctuations.

For the communication perspective, it is appropriate to describe the punctuations which the agents in an interaction use to achieve coherence and coordination, and to explain the sequence of events on the basis of those punctuations.

The interaction among development agents contains a "block" which recur,; a pattern which is structured by the interaction itself but which seems—to the participants—to take on a life of its own.

Such unwanted repetitive patterns have been studied in other contexts; for example, see Cronen, Pearce, and Snavely (1979). These patterns suggest the question: Why do the participants not simply walk away from them? The answer lies in the degree of enmeshment, or the extent to which the participants are sincerely committed to each other and to a common task.

In our analysis, each of the development agents has reasons for complaining about the interaction in which he is involved, but the reasons differ for each agent. Further, the reasons pertain to the interaction as a whole, not to the unilateral acts of any particular agent. In chapter 9, we make some recommendations about what might be done to reduce the amount of discontent being experienced by development agents—or make the discontent more tolerable.

NINE

Administration and Public Policy in Communication

THE "COMMUNICATION PERSPECTIVE" led us to examine development in India in a manner unusual in this literature. We focused on the actual sequence of acts in the interaction among planners, change agents, and masses; the "social realities" which guided their interpretations of and responses to those acts; and the reflexive effects that the pattern of interaction had on the agents. The results describe a major problem for development and suggest the lines of response to it.

The pattern of interaction described in chapter 8 was not intended by any of the agents who participated in it, and is inimical to the objective of self-sustaining development. Further, it has made all of the agents discontented.

The social realities of the participants enmesh them deeply within it. Their concepts of themselves, of each other, and of development itself prevent them from simply leaving or ignoring the pattern. However, the most striking finding of this study is the homeostatic stability of the pattern. None of the agents seems able to change the pattern through unilateral action. Indeed, the history of development in India shows that each of the agents has tried to change the pattern at various times, but that these efforts themselves have reconstituted the same pattern even more powerfully.

These findings are clear but their implications are puzzling. For self-sustaining development to occur, the pattern of interaction among planners, change agents, and the masses must be changed. However, that pattern is robustly homeostatic. The harder the planners, change agents, or masses *try* to change it, the more rigidly they will perpetuate it.

If that is the case, can the pattern be changed?

This chapter presents a set of specific recommendations and a Dialogue Action Strategy (DAS) that might interrupt the pattern in which the interaction among the planners, change agents, and masses is stuck and allow it to continue to evolve. These recommendations and the DAS are based on a radical rethinking of the problem, consistent with the communication perspective described in chapter 3.

In our judgment, the most rigorous and imaginative efforts— *as long as they occur within the current social realities of the development agents*—have no hope of altering the distressing, dysfunctional pattern that exists. To the contrary, they will simply "feed" the pattern and make it stronger. The only hope for change derives from a novel way of thinking—or from some fortunate accident.

Reconceptualizing a problem is far from a trivial response to an unwanted situation. Bateson (1979) observed that the way people think (their "epistemology" in his terms) shapes their actions and thus controls their destiny. A false epistemology, he wrote, is the pathway to hell. In the same vein, Harre (1983) claimed that the most insidious enemy of good government is "bad psychology." Everyone has a "theory" of psychology, he explained, composed of the way they think about themselves and each other and their concepts of duty, honor, and motivation. Whether consciously or not, people treat each other on the basis of their theories of psychology. If they have a "bad psychology," they treat each other badly and build social institutions that abuse human values and human beings.

In this sense, the social realities of the participants in the development interaction contain some "bad psychology" and some false epistemology. Specifically, rather than thinking in terms of their interaction, the agents think of themselves and each other as separate individuals, each of whom has certain quantities of motivation and competence. For example, distressed by the way development is going, they blame each other for being lazy, serving vested interests, failing to deliver what they promised, and other assorted failings.

A desirable alternative is to focus on the interaction itself, thinking of it as the product of the "fit" or intermeshing of the actions of all of the agents. By shifting attention to conjoint social patterns rather than individual acts, they are free to see that the "logic of interaction" may be unwanted by all participants, although "caused" by the particular combination of actions that—within each agent's social reality—are all appropriate and competent.

The difference between these perspectives can be seen in a comparison of the explanations of discontent and a description of the problems of low motivation. Using a "bad psychology" that focuses on individuals instead of on the interactions among them, development agents explain their discontent by saying that "we" acted reasonably but "they" frustrated the development effort because of their many vices. Taking the communication perspective, on the other hand, discontented development agents would offer accounts like this: "The manner in which our actions intermeshed frustrated development". They might even go on to say that all of the development agents did what they each thought was best for development, but they failed to achieve a desirable pattern of coordinated behavior.

The lack of motivation for development efforts is frequently cited as a problem. From the perspective of a bad psychology, motivation is seen as something individuals possess in some quantity. If they have "too little" motivation, then they should be trained, exhorted, or somehow persuaded to be "more" motivated. From the communication perspective, motivation is not seen as a substance possessed in particular quantities. Rather, the social structure—comprised of the patterns of social interactions—affords individuals opportunities to act in some ways and not in others. Shotter (1984) suggests that if the social structure affords conviction, power, and the delivery of goods, the individual will act in ways we call "highly motivated." However, the interaction among development agents does not contain such "affordances," and thus the agents act in ways often, but misleadingly, explained as the result of their having "insufficient" (whatever that means) motivation.

In a real sense, rather than being "taken" by the actor, one's identity (e.g., as a professional change agent) and the meaning of one's actions (e.g., giving advice) are "given" by the social group with which one interacts. If the social interaction does not "afford" a particular role, then it is difficult—if not impossible—for any agent to "take" it. There is *no* set of actions the planners can *take themselves* that will fit their desired role as "expert distributors of scarce governmental resources to the grateful and actively participating masses."

All too often in the history of development efforts in India, we have seen agents who attempted to "take" particular meanings for their actions, and who were frustrated because other agents responded in undesired ways. Within conventional manners of thinking, the appropriate, even noble response to such frustration is to try harder, to do more of the same, and to persevere. Our analysis of the interaction pattern, however, shows that tenacity can be—and in this case is—self-defeating.

We urge a new way of thinking about development that focuses on the interaction among the agents. There are two reasons for taking this radical step. First, it is more accurate. Our analyses in chapters 4, 5, and 6 have shown that there is no single "villain" in the history of Indian development. Within their own social realities, each category of agents has for the most part acted honorably and responsibly to achieve development. For any agent to explain his development discontents by alleging that the others are "mad, bad, or sick" is simply wrong.

Second, this radical reconceptualization enables effective action in a way not available without it. From this perspective, strategies and recommendations can be framed within a vocabulary that describes patterns of interaction rather than, for example, praise and blame for particular agents. It is these vocabularies of praise and blame that produce the dilemmas, binds, and dependencies described in chapters 5, 6, and 7, and within those vocabularies, no lines of effective action are possible.

The reconceptualization we suggest is subtle, and contradicts much of the conventional wisdom about social action and the evaluation of national programs. We do not expect that it should be conveyed to the planners, masses, or change agents by descriptive argument. Rather, we propose a series of specific action recommendations and a Dialogue Action Strategy. Implementation of these will place development agents into situations in which they will naturally think in a manner consistent with the "communication perspective."

DYSFUNCTIONS OF DEVELOPMENT PROGRAMS

It is important for development agents to know why the pattern of interaction that has occurred has been so dissatisfying. If they are not to blame each other, then what explanation is possible?

It is scarcely satisfactory to say that the pattern is accidental, the unintended result of the uncoordinated, best efforts of multiple agents with compatible goals but incommensurate social realities. This account leaves unanswered the questions of why the social realities of the agents differed in just these ways, and why this particularly stable, unwanted pattern resulted from their interaction.

Our analysis of the three development decades reveals knowable reasons. The interaction pattern that has made all development agents discontented was not predestined, but it was prefigured by historical factors involving political leadership, development administration, and the rural and urban masses.

The government's goal—achieving self-sustaining development that improves the material well-being of the masses within a context of democratic socialism—is particularly difficult, and contains some unresolved contradictory tensions. Success would require a highly sophisticated coordination of people's participation, local leadership, and effective administration. As shown in Figure 9.1, this coordination was not achieved. The "affordances" of the social system resulted in weak local leadership, ineffective functionaries in the development bureaucracy, and masses who remained dependent, although they shifted their dependence from the local community to the central government.

Our analysis shows that the social structure has changed in the villages during the three development decades, in part because of the success of development communication programs. Among other things, this implies that the communication strategies that were successful at one phase of development have made themselves inappropriate. Further, our data show that the rural and rurban social structures differ markedly, and that the communication strategies designed for rural programs are relatively ineffective in rurban areas.

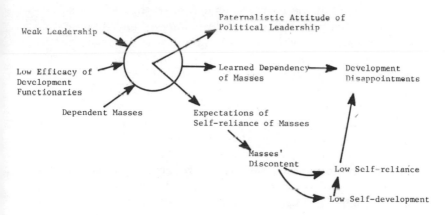

Figure 9.1. Dysfunctional factors in development.

Both of these findings combine to contradict the conventional wisdom that there is a universal communication strategy to meet the development needs of all sections of the society. In fact, the use of development communication strategies that do not fit the local community are themselves a source of discontent.

Applications of Policy Skills
Toward Development Efforts

The interaction among development agents is produced by all of the agents, and none can change the pattern by unilateral action. However, it is also true that the planners and administrators have the opportunity to initiate changes. They have the material resources and, more importantly, the advantages of cognitive flexibility acquired through education and exposure to other cultures.

In this section, we make a series of recommendations about three of the most serious problems with the current pattern of development interaction: pervasive discontent, perceived helplessness, learned dependency.

Discontent and Perceived Helplessness

Virtually all of the participants described themselves as helpless to achieve the objectives of development, and discontented with the extent to which development objectives are achieved. Discontent and a feeling of personal inefficacy are serious concerns for development, not just a matter of sentiment, because they make people blame each other and withdraw from commitment to democratic participation in development.

Development functionaries have blamed the masses: Planners think of them as helpless to participate effectively in planning and implementing development projects, administrators fear they are becoming too dependent on government handouts, and contact agents find them demanding but unwilling to take the initiative. On the other hand, the masses blame the government: Contact agents are perceived as partial to vested interests and inadequate means of expressing messages upward in the development hierarchy, administrators are perceived as indifferent, and planners are seen as caring and well-intentioned, but unable for some reason to deliver the goods and services they promise to the people. These patterns of reciprocated blaming wreck the kind of coordination necessary to achieve development objectives.

Pervasive discontent with the development program itself is usually thought of as a "problem" which should be eliminated if possible, and it is a problem if it leads to a withdrawal from participation in development programs. But discontent need not be—and need not be thought of—as problematic.

We recommend that *discontent be treated as an inevitable, valuable aspect of democratic development, not as a problem about which some solution should be sought.* This suggestion recognizes Maslow's (1971) contention that people always "grumble." Participants in the development interaction should be taught that discontent is natural and a symptom of healthy development, not an unnatural correlate of problems. They should accept discontent and see it as a good thing rather than as a reason to withdraw from the development interaction or to seek "solutions."

Consider the implications of development without discontent. Discontent is consistently expressed in terms of frustration at the inability to achieve the goals of development, not only the immediate goals of an acceptable rate of adoption of a particular innovation but the broader and longer range goals of restructuring the society in a more just manner.

There are two ways in which this discontent could be reduced, but both of them are undesirable.

One "solution" is to abandon the goal of democratic socialism and the tensions it inherently creates between expertise and democracy, between short-term efficiency and long-term effectiveness. This could be done by writing off the poor as unreachable, unsavable, and incapable of active participation in a democratic government. The goal of development could be changed to that of making the elites more comfortable or of making the national economy a more industrial one and letting the benefits trickle down through the social structure. With such "lower"—or at least more easily reached—standards, "success" is easier and discontent less likely.

This result is, of course, only a possibility. But even entertaining the notion of lowering development objectives suggests a way of rethinking discontent among development agents. The very pervasiveness of discontent is a symptom of an unswerving commitment to the highest development objectives.

A second "solution" is to impose patterns of activity and meaning on other groups, for example, by setting agricultural production quotas and forcibly confiscating those amounts from farmers. This procedure provides a strong motivation for agricultural innovation but destroys the possibility of a partnership between the people and the government. Sanctions like this were used in the "development" effort in the Soviet Union and in the Peoples' Republic of China. This "solution" betrays the mandate of the Indian government as a democracy, even if it might reduce the frustration and discontent of development personnel.

Both of these "solutions" to discontent involve evading some aspect of the responsibilities entailed by the concept of democratic socialism. Within this concept of the nation, there is no "solution" to discontent and the search for one is misguided and counterproductive. To the contrary, participants in the development interaction should accept discontent, as an inevitable phenomenon with which they must cope.

The *potential* for discontent is an inherent feature of any democratic interaction, since no participant has unilateral power to control the emerging pattern. The patterns of interaction often do not resemble the intentions of any participant—sometimes to their delight and sometimes to their consternation. Several historical features make discontent with development practically unavoidable in a democracy.

The government commitment to development required mutually exclusive practices from the beginning. As a result, political leaders and planners could not be fully content with anything they did, since whatever satisfied one set of demands undercut the other.

At Independence, the masses were unable to participate in, much less initiate, development efforts. They were fatalistically resigned to the status quo, unaware of alternatives, opposed to change as a matter of principle, ensnared in local exploitative linkages, and unaccustomed to cooperating with other communities and the central government. The "romantic" concept of the masses as full partners with the government in development—a concept to which the government was formally committed—was politically necessary but unrealistic. Consistent with this concept, however, much of the effort during the first decade was an attempt to implement a fully participatory program of development. The next three five-year plans—while preserving at least some of the rhetoric praising participation—consisted of a much more centralized program to redesign rural social structure and deliver development benefits directly to the weakest sections of society. The sixth five-year Plan explicitly endorses both a highly centralized procedure in which the government assumes responsibility and a participatory model in which the government declines the responsibility for making development work.

This sequence sets up a "charmed loop" in which the government takes perpetual responsibility. Since the government decided that it was its task to make the people ready for participation in development, any failure by the people implies that the government is at fault for not successfully preparing them, and thus they should double their efforts. There is no "exit" from this loop because there is no criterion for adequate "readiness." The more effort the government expends, the more they perceive whatever condition the masses are in as the result of their efforts, not as a condition the masses have achieved which equips them to work autonomously.

The relationship between the government and the people is sensitive because it involves "trust." Trust involves three components: to trust someone, you must perceive them as well-intentioned toward you, knowledgable about the consequences of their actions toward you, and capable of performing the acts they choose (Rossiter and Pearce, 1975). When the other is performing specific acts you have taught them, it is difficult to trust them because their autonomy has been compromised; you cannot tell whether they are performing desirable acts because you have taught them to or because they are trustworthy. The usual tendency is to attribute their performance to your instruction and/or close surveillance rather than to their trustworthiness—that is, to suppose that if you had not been exhorting them to perform well or closely inspecting them, their "true nature" would have emerged and they would have performed badly. The phenomenon is a high inverse correlation between surveillance and trust.

We have no easy "solution" to discontent in the sense of some magic formula that will make it go away. But we may have something better than a solution: some ways of coping with the situation. One way of coping is expressed in our first recommendation, that discontent be seen as an inevitable aspect of democratic development in a country not initially ready for participatory decentralization. Many sages have noted that persons can bear any amount of pain or discomfort as long as they know why they must. We suggest that the discontent with development is more bearable if seen—accurately—as a symptom of a commitment to the most noble, long-range objectives.

There are some other ways of dealing with discontent: reducing but not eliminating it. These are discussed in the context of other recommendations.

Learned Dependency

Unlike discontent, which must be borne (perhaps proudly), the masses' learned dependency on the government must be changed. We have a complex set of recommendations, all of which are based on the analysis of a continuing interaction between the government and the people.

We recommend that *development communication include explicit statements about the relationship between government and people* as well as information and exhortation about particular development projects. The realization that communication is more important, is more complex, and has more subtle effects than had been thought sets an agenda for much more resourceful and innovative uses of communication. One way of realizing this agenda is to include metacommunication as part of development communication.

Every aspect of the development interaction functions as a message, whether intended that way or not, about the relationship between the participants. Setting up the Panchyat Raj or electing a party whose campaign slogan is "Remove Poverty" are powerful—if not necessarily eloquent—statements about that relationship. Our recommendation is to make some of these statements more eloquent, not simply because eloquence is "nice" but because the history of this interaction demands a carefully articulated statement.

The type of statement we envision consists of a development communication program comparable in form to those directed to particular social innovations. The content of this program, however, is the development interaction itself, and it should have three features.

1. It should directly address the context in which this and other development programs occur. This requires educating the masses to see development as an interaction leading to partnership with the government. The goal of development as a "people's program with government participation" can be acknowledged, and they can be taught to see particular plans and actions as statements about the relationships among the participants. That is, it should teach them a bit of the "communication perspective."

2. It should acknowledge the contradictory messages the masses have received in the past and provide a way of interpreting them that does not lead to learned dependency. This is crucial, because the masses have a right to be confused. At one time, they were invited to be a full participant in development, but they had little reason to believe that their participatory acts were heard or taken into consideration. Then they were given mixed messages, but rather clearly told that they were incapable of making a contribution to development. After that, they were told that the failure of development is their fault because they have not been sufficiently active in their participation with development. It is not surprising that they do not approve of the way development has been handled, or that they now are willing to allow the government to take all responsibility for it.

3. It should explain the contradictory messages received in the past as the expression of two incompatible tasks that must occur in a particular sequence. Sometimes the government was trying to implement a fully participatory program and said one thing, and at other times trying to make the local communities ready to participate and said another. This program should not be afraid to say that the government made mistakes and expressed itself unclearly. A telling of the story of the interaction comparable to the analysis presented in chapter 8 would be fully consistent with democratic traditions and would enable various agents in the interaction to understand why they have found themselves in confusing or frustrating positions.

207

We recommend that *development planning explicitly include two categories of programs, one for local communities ready for active participation, the other for those that are not.* This recommendation envisions a plan similar to the sixth, with an important difference. Rather than mixing two incompatible approaches—the centralized basic mimimum needs model and the decentralized participatory approach—this would clearly structure them as two very different plans running simultaneously but for different communities.

To implement this plan, a program of social education would be conducted, first for the development bureaucracy and then for the masses, announcing a new program designed to cooperate with the rural elite, but only on the basis of community organization and local contributions.

To show eligibility for the program, the community would have to demonstrate "active participation." A community ready for participation would submit its own descriptions of its needs, give a priority ranking of them, and match government contributions with its own contributions (e.g., a list of who in the community will contribute what labor, cash, or kind). In addition, they would have to show how the weaker sections of the community would be advantaged—or at least not harmed—by the proposed projects.

These communities would receive a very different—and substantially more attractive—package of government efforts than a community not yet ready for development. In this way, the government can continue its efforts to reach the weakest sections of society directly, and do so in a way that does not lead to learned dependence by the stronger sections.

To make this recommendation effective, two features should be present. First, *the program for local communities ready for participation should be substantially more attractive than that for those not ready.* This may seem unfair but is necessary to provide a positive motivation for communities to pledge themselves to active participation. The "ethic of proportional effort" will prevent the effectiveness of this program unless some answer is given to the question, "Why should I donate some of my own resources when the people in other communities do not have to?" It would be convenient to pass legislation forbidding people from thinking in a way so incompatible with democratic socialism, but, realistical, the program must provide an inducement to show that active participation in projects that will result in the common good are also in the best selfish interests of the rural elite.

To avoid resistance and resentment from the masses in communities not yet ready for participation, the development communication program described above must be effective in teaching the people that this is a phased sequence, not a discrimination in favor of better-developed communities. Appropriate symbolisms can surely be selected to avoid some unfortunate interpretations.

Second, *the decision whether a community is ready for participation should be made by that community.* This feature is the key that makes the whole package work. Given the history of the interaction, virtually anything the government tries to "say" to the masses is likely to be interpreted as "experts telling us what to do"—an interpretation which increases dependency in a parent-child relationship. One way to escape that interpretation is for the government to say that because of its expertise and experience, it has learned that only the local community can decide whether it is ready for phase two of the development interaction. If the local community says nothing, the government will continue as best it can to provide the benefits of development to the weakest sections of the community and to restructure the social system to remove impediments to development. But when the community is ready, it can inform the government of its desire to participate in phase two by presenting its demands with a priority listing and by initiating the community contribution to the specific projects described. The message that only the local community can decide when it is ready for participatory development should be a major part of the development communication program described above.

The government probably will not want to surrender to the local elites all the responsibility for planning, but it must avoid the appearance of acting in a parental manner. One approach is to structure the "application" for phase two status in such a manner that the local community must attend to appropriate matters in filling out the application. In this way, the government can take the role of "helper" in the preparation of local plans more than as the "judge" of completed plans. For instance, part of the application could be detailed plans that have appended the advice and recommendations of some appropriately trained expert (e.g., an engineer's technical assessment of plans for a bridge to be built).

This package of recommendations does several desirable things:

1. In their efforts to prepare communities for participation, the planners and administrators have a criterion for "success" they can trust. The activity by which the community declares its readiness for participatory development should include a good deal of participation, and should be conducted without the close supervision or surveillance of the administrators. In this way, the government's response to the "readiness" of the community is a recognition of a fait accompli, not a prediction of things to come.

2) This approach gets the local communities actively involved in planning in a way that does not require great technical competence. In rurban and urban areas, it may require the creation of desirable local community structures.

3) Having the responsibility to make their own decision changes the whole thrust of the development interaction up to this point for the masses. Rather than being told they are helpless or technically incompetent—or even that a parental expert has decided they are belatedly brought to the point where they can be entrusted with some responsibility—the masses are told that only *they* can decide the extent to which they are ready for participatory development. The task of making the decision, or even of thinking in those terms, involves the masses in a more active manner.

This package of recommendations places some new burdens on the development bureaucracy, and this requires some consideration.

DEVELOPMENT ADMINISTRATION INFRASTRUCTURE

Because the development experience as a whole *is* (rather than contains) a process of communication, the organization and functioning of the administrative bureaucracy is a part of the construction of social reality about development. As such, specific attention should be given to administrative matters not only in terms of organizational charts and the like, but in terms of the way it functions as a participant in the development interaction. Our reading of the progression of this interaction suggests three concerns: the development of administrative plans, timely evaluation of administrative performance, the creation of a special administrative cadre for development.

Administrative Plans

A persistent complaint among participants in development is that the administrators are indifferent, that they do not take the time to investigate and redress problems, and so forth. Our study of administrators found that they perceive themselves as having too many responsibilities, sometimes without specific training for development and without sufficient resources and time to meet all the needs expressed to them by the people. They also feel themselves rendered helpless by their dependence on contact agents, whom they do not trust to implement development projects fairly or even to take appropriate initiative in meeting the felt needs of the people.

For example, the Delhi Development Authority is a housing agency. Its normal function is planning and constructing houses in Delhi. Their responsibility for rurban resettlement colonies such as Jhangirpuri is primarily to plan and construct the physical aspects of the community. However, the people have come to expect them to serve as the government representative for all development functions. As the story of the latrine sweepers shows, they have become the employers of maintenance personnel, and are held accountable by the people for a broad spectrum of government services. This is a role for which their experience as a housing agency has not prepared them. They have often done well but only because they have been able to adapt to novel task demands, not because there is a development infrastructure providing them training, staff and resources.

We recommend that *the plans for development be accompanied by a counterpart plan of administrative development and evaluation, making the structure of the development bureaucracy commensurate with the rationale and materials of current programs.* During the history of development in India, a number of modernizations have been implemented in administrative systems and procedures, but there has been no basic change in the overall patterns of personnel management or administrative structure. We believe that there should be such a plan, based on an assessment of the administrative needs of particular development programs. The plan should include specific proposals for developing the required administrative capabilities. The necessary administrative capabilities may sometimes require the establishment of a new organizational structure; at other times it may require the continuing, adequate training of personnel already in existing organizations.

Our data show that the social structure in rurban areas differs from that of rural and urban communities, and thus the administrative requirements of comparable development plans differ among these communities. The DDA is poorly equipped to handle the specific development functions in Jhangirpuri and other resettlement colonies. If development objectives are set for rurban areas, the plan should contain proposals for the necessary development administration infrastructure. For example, block development infrastructures used for rural areas have never been employed in rurban communities. Perhaps some comparable structure should be developed, or perhaps some novel structure based on the specific characteristics of the community.

Our data also show that the block development personnel at times did not have adequate training to handle the development problems of the masses. As a result, the people perceive the administrators as ineffective, and the administators feel handicapped by their lack of training. This is particularly vexing for contact agents, who are expected to be able to handle many of the complaints addressed to them by the people but do not feel sufficiently trained. They then pass on the complaints to the program directors or block development officials, who feel overwhelmed by the quantity of complaints and resent the contact agents for not dealing with more of them. During the time the extension model was the guide, considerable attention was given to the training of contact agents. However, in recent years this training has been neglected. It should be reinstated as part of a participatory model.

The necessary training is not limited to technical matters. The administrators should be participants in the development communication program described, treating the history of development as an interaction. They should be taught that their performance in office is a statement to the people, and should be trained to work in such a way as to make their statements compatible with the objectives of the larger plan. Part of each periodic plan should be a clearly defined statement the plan itself makes to the people, and the administrators should have this statement carefully explained to them so they can pass it on to the people and conduct themselves in such a way as to reinforce that message.

For example, the "message" given to the people under the sixth plan is fundamentally contradictory. The contradiction comes in part because the planners have simultaneously endorsed incompatible models, but a more troublesome aspect of contradiction comes from the discrepancy between what is said to the people by the planners by means of mass media and by the administrators and contact agents in person. The planners say in effect, "We will take responsiblity"; while the administrators and change agents tell the masses, in effect, "It's your fault that development has not worked, because you have not assumed responsiblity." Learned dependency is one result of this incompatibility between the statements made—probably unintentionally—by various government personnel.

Administrative Evaluations

The concept of program evaluation is certainly not new. Many of the major points in the development interaction took the form of assessments of the extent to which development objectives were achieved. However, virtually all of the current evaluations focus on the success or failure of specific projects based on the response of the masses.

We recommend that *development personnel be evaluated in terms of the way they are perceived by the masses with whom they work* as well as by objective criteria and normal institutional performance standards. This recommendation is based on the conviction that the reciprocated perception of the masses and the contact agents and administrators is not merely an addendum to development but is a central feature. Our research shows that the primary setting for development communication is face-to-face interaction between the masses and the contact agents, and that the "meaning" of development is closely related to the reciprocal perceptions these persons have of each other.

Our data also indicate that administrators and change agents are cruelly limited by a lack of specific knowledge and training about the development projects they are handling. The notion that any generalist administrator can administer any special development project is largely at fault. As a result of this notion, people are assigned to projects about which they have little specific knowledge, and this constrains their ability to function effectively. We recommend that *personnel evaluation focus on the specific knowledge and training required by particular development projects*.

The point that we are making is not that there is now no program of personnel evaluation within the administrative services, but that these programs are considered as only a matter of personnel evaluations. They are not considered a vital component of the development effort, but they should be. An important aspect of these evaluations should be the masses' perceptions of their administrative performance.

We recommend that *the organizational arrangements of the devleopment infrastructure be periodically evaluated.* One recurring complaint about the block development office is that there are too many levels of administration through which any message must pass before any action can be taken. This causes inordinate delays in responding to the masses' demands; worse, it produces changes in the meaning of messages as they go up or down the multiple layers of hierarchy, or outright informational blockages.

Another recurring complaint is that these organizations have insufficient operational and financial autonomy. The administrators cite political pressures (unrelated to the development effort) that force them to perform official behaviors which are not only distasteful but counterproductive to their development activities.

A Professional Development Cadre

We recommend that *a special administrative development cadre be set up specifically to train administrators for handling development projects.*

COMMUNICATION INFRASTRUCTURE

Communication is a situated activity in which each agent becomes the context for the other, and in which the characteristics of the environment channel the interaction into particular patterns. Persons seek to coordinate their activities with others and participate in ongoing interactions on the basis of their interpretations of the meaning of the event up to the present point. These interpretations, however, are strongly influenced by the habitual patterns of communication and the availability of channels for receiving or sending messages.

Our data indicate that the development interaction has taken some unfortunate patterns because of the deficiences in the communication infrastructure. These deficiences have substituted infrequent and inadequate feedback for the dialogue that should occur.

The infrastructure is well developed in terms of getting messages to the masses from the government, and has some capacity for getting feedback from the masses to the government. However, feedback is a unidirectional message flow from the masses to the government. The masses are not at all sure they have been heard, and if heard, understood; and if understood, taken seriously; and if taken seriously, acknowledged as the cause of government action. The most frequent responses to their feedback are disclaimers from the change agents (who say they passed the message on through proper channels and do not know what is happening to it now) and inferences from public pronouncements on mass media by the government, general messages usually not specifically related to the complaint or suggestion. Having one's messages vanish into the bureaucracy without trace is an insurmountable obstacle to the development of a sense of efficacy and involvement.

The concept of participatory development, as well as democratic socialism, suggests that dialogue should replace feedback; not only must the communication patterns be two-way, they must be fully interactive. But this poses great practical problems in a country as populous and diverse as India. Obviously, genuine dialogue cannot occur everywhere, since the planning commission cannot sit down with the residents of every village. But dialogue can be productively approximated by carefully planned activities.

We recommend that *dialogue be created by Dialogue Action Strategies* (DAS). Some characteristics of DAS projects are required by the specific characteristics of the communities in which they occur. We note some of these characteristics in the following paragraphs; a proposal for a DAS project is presented later in the chapter.

One characteristic is the existence of interpersonal contact points in communities where they do not now exist. Our data show that rural communities have ample interpersonal channels, whereas rurban and urban communities do not. We have previously recommended the development of administrative infrastructure for these communities. One phase of the responsibility of these organizations would be devising means by which the residents of these communities could be brought into contact with development personnel.

A second characteristic is the two-way use of media. Radio forums and teleclubs have proven a fruitful way of approximating dialogue in rural areas. This procedure should be explored for new applications and introduction to new areas.

Our reading of the history of development in India indicates that the government has done a commendable job in identifying and disrupting local social structures that isolate particular groups from the economy or from the flow of development information. Our data show an important remaining social obstruction. There is a development gap for women.

There are no adequate development communication networks for women. They feel that the males in the community, as well as male contact agents and block development officers, impede the flow of information to them, both by habit and by social practices. Because they have been blocked from development information, the women in our samples felt they had lost many development opportunities and were lagging far behind the men in development.

The women are not given adequate opportunities for participation in development processes. For example, they are underrepresented in block development offices, and the government recommendations for women village-level workers and women opinion leaders have not been implemented adequately. They felt they had no way to get their complaints and development priorities expressed to the government, so that in the overall local development plans, their priorities are ignored. For example, in Lampur, the priority expressed by the male-dominated local leadership was for agricultural innovations and training at a time when the women were more concerned about the distance they had to travel to get drinking water and cooking fuel. Their priorities were water taps in the houses and a biogas plant in the village. The women felt left out of consideration for training. Either they were excluded, as from the agricultural training programs, or limited to programs that featured only relatively unremunerative domestic skills. The women in our samples felt that the government was ignoring women. We recommend that *ways be found to bring women fully into the development process.*

An Integrated Approach to Development Communication

We recommend an integrated approach to development that subsumes various interconnected and interdependent dimensions of development under a single, comprehensive program. This recommendation endorses an idea currently receiving much attention by Indian analysts, and is based on the experience of the sixth plan.

The sixth five-year Plan recognized the plurality of independent programs as a problem, and devised a strategy of Integrated Rural Development (IRD). The IRD stipulates planning that includes all of the people within a given geographic area: men and women, elite and poor, etcetera.

We suggest two extensions of this good idea. First, it should be extended across the programs in a given geographic area. The problems identified as objectives of development efforts are themselves interrelated, and the solutions to them cannot be applied in a piecemeal fashion. For example, "health" cannot be provided simply by building medical facilities, because health also involves nutrition, and that in turn involves concern about the availability of food, changes in diet, agricultural techniques and supplies, transportation of products to markets, employment and wages sufficient to purchase foods and medicines, and more.

Second, integrated planning should include urban and rurban areas as well as rural. One consequence of rural development is urban migration, which creates a new problem: urban poor, many of whom have rural backgrounds.

Whether rural, rurban, or urban, an integrated development approach enables a planned balance of mass communication and interpersonal communication channels. The balancing ratio may depend on six factors: 1) the type of operative development programs; 2) various characteristics of the masses to be reached and the sections of the society involved, such as rural/rurban/ urban, male/female, and literate/illiterate; 3) the developent orientation of the masses; 4) the cultural values of the people; 5) the geographic and physical characteristics of the area; 6) available technological and economic resourses.

Two considerations are particularly important in planning a communication "channel mix." First, the channels must be easily accessible to the people. The mere existence of a communication channel does not necessarily imply that it will have any value for development. Our data show that some channels have technological limitations and others are blocked because of the social structure. Second, the channels should be "interactive" in nature, permitting not only a two-way flow of messages but some way for both sides to know that their messages have been heard.

The development experience has taught us that *greater use of mass communication may be unproductive* for various reasons. First, mass communication channels are not necessarily effective means of reaching the poor. For various physical, technological, economic and social reasons, an increase in messages on these channels may not result in any improvement in the pattern of interaction among development agents. Second, the available technological capacities of these channels are underutilized. India has invested heavily in satellite communication technology but at present is using much of this capacity to broadcast American entertainment programs. The effect of "I Love Lucy," "Star Trek," and "Different Strokes" in facilitating development of the rural poor is as yet not firmly established. Such programming suits the purposes of sponsors because it appeals to the tastes of the affluent, cosmopolitan urban elites, but is broadcast by means of the satellite to the rural populations as well. Third, as utilized, these channels are for the most part noninteractive. Fourth, the masses perceive some mass communication channels as not very credible. Fifth, the repetition of messages on the mass communication channels soon leads to satiation.

In much the same way, the development experience suggests that *greater use of existing interpersonal channels of communication is unproductive*. For various reasons, change agents and local elites tend to block the vertical flow of information between the masses and the administrators. The horizontal networks of communication among friends and family are more open, but less rich in information about development.

Dialogue Action Strategies

Dialogue Action Strategies are designed to interrupt the existing pattern of interaction and allow another, preferable one to evolve. The purpose of these strategies is to involve all of the development agents, to circumvent the spiral of reciprocal blame, and to provide social structures that afford development agents conviction, power, and the delivery of goods.

In combination with the recommendations offered above, we suggest a process to involve administrative and contact change agents and the masses in focused, problem-solving, face-to-face communication. The overall purpose is to provide a forum in which each group is involved with each other in a task-oriented context.

There may be any number of ways in which dialogue can be implemented. The following is specifically tailored for a rurban colony like Jhangirpuri or a progressive village like Lampur. It consists of a sequence of three meetings among development agents, each of which has a specified agenda. It is less important that these agendas be followed than that the groups who are meeting decide for themselves whether to follow them.

Step 1: A voluntary community group, a self-selected group from the masses, meets with the development functionaries involved with particular, ongoing development programs. The purpose of this meeting is to teach the development agents about the nature of the interaction among them, to allow all participants to express their complaints, and to permit all participants to hear the complaints others make against them. Each group should include no more than twenty-five persons, and there may be any number of such groups who meet.

This meeting should begin with the screening of a film that depicts the interaction among development agents. Actors representing the masses, change agents, and planners should portray the interaction as diagrammed in Chapter 8, and deal with some specific topic, such as the pond in Lampur or the latrines in Jhangirpuri.

Following the film, a carefully trained discussion leader should initiate discussion by asking questions of the audience. In each case, he or she should use the "circular questioning technique" in which one agent is asked how a second acts toward a third. For example, change agents would be asked to what extent the masses in the film acted toward each other or the planners like the masses in the community in which the meeting is being held. Each of the groups represented would be asked to whom each of the others shows their discontent, and in what manner.

This form of discussion requires each member of the group to consider his or her own actions as they are perceived by others, and to express how another group thinks and acts toward a third. It should be allowed to happen before each group begins to express its own complaints about the others.

Step 2: In a second meeting of each group, the participants are invited to describe particular problems for which they seek solutions, and to offer solutions, no matter how wild and unreasonable they might be. This is a form of brainstorming, in which everyone has a chance to explore alternatives and no one can veto another's ideas.

Step 3: The third meeting is designed to select one of the solutions and describe its implementation. The necessity of selecting a particular line of action is the key to this proposal because it makes the participants look beyond their blame for each other and the irritations which are bound to occur in these discussions.

These meetings should take place in quick succession, perhaps a week apart.

The results expected from the Dialogue Action Strategies include the following:

1. There is a bit of "reality testing," in which various development agents have a chance to express themselves to, and listen to, other groups. Our study shows that groups blame each other for frustrating goals of development, but they do not know the complaints the others have against them.

2. There is an improved exchange of information. Our study suggests that development programs initiated by administrators are often rejected by the people as not being relevant to their needs, and the demands of the people are rejected by the administrators as being impractical, requiring unavailable resources, etcetera.

3. Practical difficulties of implementing the program are more likely to be identified because there is cooperation between the local residents and the planners and administrators.

4. Face-to-face interaction among the change agents is likely to lead them to replace "bad psychology" with concepts that focus on interaction, thus reconceptualizing their whole development experience in a productive manner.

The Dialogue Action Strategies resemble in some ways the Communication Action Plans (CAP) currently being proposed by some members of the international development community. These CAP programs emphasize three dimensions of the participatory paradigm: self-development, self-reliance, active participation. They insist that the communities plan their own need-based programs, that they use their own resources, and that they act on their own plans.

These are laudable objectives, but given the particular history of development in India, any message from the planners or administrators that says just this will be subsumed into and perpetuate the existing pattern of interaction. In India, "communication" about development must mean "dialogue."

The CAP proposals state that active participation should be based on the interaction between development functionaires and the masses, but so far at least these plans do not specify how that interaction should take place. Our analysis agrees that interaction is crucial, but we make the further argument that putting these people together is insufficient, because it will merely perpetuate the dysfunctional pattern that now exists. "Communication" must be converted to "dialogue"; the pattern of interaction itself must be revised if the goal is to be reached. The DAS proposal focuses on the quality of interaction, not simply its occurrence, in a multistep process leading to conjoint selection of collaborative actions that will meet development needs.

CONCLUSION

The stagnant pond outside Lampur and the uncleaned latrines of Jhangirpuri are tangible parts of the development effort in India. They are simultaneously the basis of and symbolize the complex strands of idealism and selfishness, commitment and dismay, planning and bureaucracy, blame and self-justification, and overwhelming discontent that comprise current Indian development. Our data and theoretical orientations lead us to suggest that the pond and latrines are identified as a problem—not simply an existing state of affairs—because of the success of government communication policies designed to engender discontent and motivation for a better life among the Indian masses; but that the pond and latrines remain unimproved because those very processes of communication are part of a larger pattern of interaction among change agents, planners, and the masses in which all parties blame the others and wait for the others to take decisive initiative. Our data suggest that this pattern is *stuck*: the masses have learned to be dependent on the government; the change agents are caught in dependency and distrust binds; and the planners are caught in a charmed loop of responsibility. If development is to continue, to become more efficient, and to become self-sustaining, then this pattern must somehow be interrupted.

Our analysis is in some ways unique, but in other ways it parallels the concerns of Indian development analysts and other members of the international development community. National and international forums are currently debating "integrated development," "interactive development communication strategies," "active participation," and "interactive communication" among development sources and targeted populations. The common objective of the participants in these conferences is to discover ways in which the gap between the rich and poor peoples of the world can be reduced, and goods and services can be delivered to those who need them effectively. They have come to realize that this process is historically situated and that the next wave of development efforts must take into account the history of those that have gone before, including the unintended, sometimes counterproductive effects of development activities themselves. The analysis we have presented here is intended as a contribution to those discussions.

As large and laudable as the task of development, it remains only one of the contexts of human activity. We believe that it should not be pursued as if it were isolated from other domains of scholarly inquiry. Much about the human condition can be learned from a study of how people act in development programs, just as much wisdom for development programs can be drawn from other areas of the humanities and social sciences. The still-stagnant pond outside Lampur and the perpetually uncleaned latrines of Jhangirpuri are neither discontinuous from nor all that far removed from other forms of human activity both in India and beyond.

Reference List

Adhikarya, Ronny, and Everett M. Rogers. 1978. Communication and inequitable development: Narrowing the socio-economic benefits gap. *Media Asia* 1:3–9.

Althusser, Louis. 1971. *Lenin and philosophy.* London: New Left Books.

Asian Regional Seminar on Rural Communication. 1977. *Report.* Hyderabad: Osmania University, Asia Mass Communication and Information Centre, and Indian Council of Social Science Research.

Baraghouti, S. M. 1974. The role of communication in Jordan's rural development. *Journalism Quarterly* 51:418–24.

Barnlund, Dean. 1970. A transactional model of communication. In *Foundations of communication theory*, edited by Ken Sereno and C. David Mortensen. New York: Harper and Row.

Bateson, Gregory. 1972. *Steps to an ecology of mind.* New York: Ballantine.

Beltran, L. R. 1971. Communication and domination. Paper presented to the Seminar on Channels of Social Communication and Education, Mexico City.

Berlo, David K. 1960. *The process of communication.* New York: Holt, Rinehart and Winston.

Bordenave, J. Diza. 1976. Communication of agricultural innovations in Latin America—the need for new models. In *Communication and development: Critical perspectives*, edited by E. M. Rogers. Beverly Hills: Sage.

Cohen, John M., and Norman Uphoff. 1976. *Rural development participation concepts.* Ithaca, New York: Rural Development Committee, Cornell University.

Coombs, P. H. 1980. *Meeting the basic needs of the rural poor.* New York: Pergamon.

Cronen, Vernon E., W. Barnett Pearce, and Lonna Snavely. 1979. A theory of rule structure and episode types, and a study of unwanted repetitive patterns. In *Communication yearbook III*, edited by Dan Nimmo. New Brunswick, New Jersey: Transaction.

Cronen, Vernon E., Kenneth M. Johnson, and John W. Lannamann. 1982. Paradoxes, double binds and reflexive loops: An alternative theoretical perspective. *Family Process* 20:81–112.

Dance, Frank E. X. 1970. The "concept" of communication. *Journal of Communication* 20:201–10.

Desai, M. V. 1977. *Communication policies in India.* Paris: UNESCO.

Dey, S. K. 1961. *Panchyat Raj in India.* Bombay: Asia Publishers.
———. 1962. *Nilokheri Experiment.* Bombay: Asia Publishers.

Dissanayke, Wimal. 1981. Development and communication: Four approaches. *Media Asia* 8:217–27.

Dubey, S. C. 1976. Mass media and national development. In *Communication and change in the developing countries*, edited by Wilbur Schramm and Daniel Lerner. Honolulu: University of Hawaii Press.

Ensminger, Douglas. 1972. *Rural India in transition.* Faridabad: Thompson Press.

Fay, Brian. 1975. *Social theory and political practice.* London: Allen and Unwin.

Foss, Sonja K., Karen A. Foss, and Robert Trapp. 1984. *Contemporary perspectives on rhetoric.* Prospect Heights, Illinois: Waveland Press.

Frank, A. G. 1971. *Capitalism and underdevelopment in Latin America.* London: Penguin.

Freire, Paulo. 1971. Cultural action and conscientization. *Harvard Educational Review* 40:452–78.

Galtung, Johan. 1971. *Members of two worlds: A development study of three villages in western Sicily.* New York: Columbia University Press.

Geertz, Clifford. 1975. *The interpretation of cultures*. New York: Basic Books.

Germani, G., A. Quizano, and C. Weffort. 1973. The concept of marginality. Cited in *Communication and Society* 6, edited by Ryan O'Sullivan and Mario Kaplun. 1982. Paris: UNESCO.

Giddens, Anthony. 1979. *Central problems in social theory.* London: Macmillan.

Grunig, James E. 1971. Communication and the economic decision-making process of Colombian peasants. *Economic Development and Cultural Change* 18:580–97.

Harre, Rom. 1984. *Personal being*. Cambridge: Harvard University Press.

Harris, Linda M., Alison Alexander, Sheila McNamee, Marsha Stanback, and Kyung-wha Kang. 1984. Forced cooperation: Violence as a communicative act. In *Communication theory and interpersonal interaction*, edited by Sari Thomas. Norwood, New Jersey: ABLEX Publishing Company.

Inkeles, Alex, and D. H. Smith. 1974. *Becoming modern: Individual change in six developing countries*. Cambridge: Mass.: Harvard University Press.

India since independence. 1971. New Delhi: Publication Division, Government of India.

International Labor Organization. 1976. *ILO Report*. New York: United Nations.

Jain, Sugan Chand. 1967. *Community development and Panchyat Raj in India*. New Delhi: Allied Publishers.

Janik, Alan, and Stephen Toulmin. 1973. *Wittgenstein's Vienna*. New York: Simon and Schuster.

Katz, Daniel. 1975. *Bureaucratic encounters: A pilot study in the evaluation of government services*. Ann Arbor: Institute for Social Research, University of Michigan.

Khan, Akhter Hamid. 1978. *Ten decades of rural development: Lessons learnt from India*. East Lansing: Department of Agricultural Economics, Michigan State University.

Lem, Stanislaw. 1984. *His master's voice*. New York: Harcourt Brace Jovanovich.

Lerner, Daniel. 1958. *The passing of traditional society: Modernizing the Middle East*. New York: Free Press.

Malhan, P., and Uma Narula. 1969. *Communication patterns in slums.* New Delhi: Indian Institute of Mass Communication.

Maslow, Abraham. 1971. On low grumbles, high grumbles, and metagrumbles. In *The Farther Reaches of Human Nature.* New York: Viking Press.

Masmoudi, Mustapha. 1979. The new world information order. *Journal of Communication* 29:172–85.

Mattleart, Armand. 1977. Por encima de nuestras cabezas. Mexico City: ILET Institute. Cited by Sarti, Ingrid. 1981. Communication and cultural dependency—a misconception. In *Communication and social structure,* edited by E. G. McAnany. New York: Praeger.

Mayer, Albert, with McKim Merriott and Richard L. Park. 1958. *Pilot project, India: The story of rural development at Etawah, Uttar Pradesh.* Berkeley: University of California Press.

Mehta, Prayag, and Uma Narula. 1968. *News in media.* New Delhi: Indian Institute of Mass Communication.

Minhas, B. S. 1974. *Planning and the poor.* New Delhi: S. Chand.

Ministry of Information and Broadcasting. 1971. *Annual Report.* New Delhi: Publication Division, Government of India.

Mulay, Sumati, and Uma Narula. 1972. *Satiation in family planning message receptivity.* New Delhi: Indian Institute of Mass Communication.

Muthayya, B. C. 1981. Dynamics of rural development. In *Rural development in India—some facets,* edited by S. K. Rau. Hyderabad: National Institute of Rural Development.

Narain, Iqbal, ed. 1970. *Seminar on Panchyat Raj, planning and democracy.* London: Asia Publishing House.

Narayan, Shriman. 1960. *Principles of Gandhian planning.* Allahabad: Kitab Mahal.

Narula, B. S. 1969. *Development administration.* New Delhi: Indian Institute of Public Administration.

———. 1971. *Development administration: Challenges of the 80's.* Working paper for Public Administration Unit. Bangkok: ECAFE.

Narula, Uma. 1984. Dynamics of development communication: Awareness, motivation and participation. Ph.D. dissertation. University of Massachusetts, Amherst.

Narula, Uma, and R. K. Dhawan. 1982. *Public participation in development programs—an empirical study.* New Delhi: Indian Institute of Public Administration (Delhi Chapter).

Nicholson, Norman K. 1973. *Panchyat Raj, rural development and political economy of village India.* Ithaca, New York: Rural Development Committee, Cornell University Press.

Nordenstreng, Kaarle, and Herbert Schiller. 1979. *National sovereignty and international communication.* New Jersey: ABLEX Publishing Company.

Nordenstreng, Kaarle, and Tapio Varis. 1973. Television traffic—a one-way street? A survey and analysis of international flow of TV program material. *Reports on Mass Communication 70.* Paris: UNESCO.

O'Brian, Rita C. 1974. Domination and dependence in mass communication: Implications for the use of broadcasting in developing countries. IDS Discussion Paper No. 64. University of Sussex.

O'Sullivan, Ryan J., and Mario Kaplun. 1980. Communication methods to promote grassroots participation. *Communication and Society* 6. Paris: UNESCO.

Palazzoli, Maria, Gianfranco Cecchin, Luigi Boscolo, and G. Prata. 1978. *Paradox and counterparadox.* New York: Jason, Aronson.

Pareek, Udai. 1962. A motivational paradigm of development. *Journal of Social Issues* 24:115–121.

———. 1968. Motivational patterns and planned social change. *International Social Science Journal* 20:465–73.

Pasquali, Antonio. 1975. *On the instrumental use of mass media in America for purposes of dependence.* Caracas: Universidad Central de Venezuela.

Pearce, W. Barnett, and Vernon E. Cronen. 1980. *Communication, action, and meaning: The creation of social realities.* New York: Praeger.

Pearce, W. Barnett, and Kim Andrew Elliott. 1983. Putting the right "concepts" in the right "order." *Intermedia* 11:15–19.

Ploman, E. W. 1979. Development approaches and implications for communication policy. Paper presented to the Seminar on Rural Development and Communication Policies, Hyderabad.

Raghvan, G. N. S. 1976. Development Communication-research report. New Delhi: Indian Institute of Mass Communication.

Report of the team for study of community projects and NES committee on plan projects. 1957. New Delhi: Government of India.

Rogers, Everett M. 1962. *Diffusion of innovations.* New York: Free Press.

————. 1976. *Communication and development: Critical perspectives.* Beverly Hills: Sage.

————. 1983. *Diffusion of innovations,* 3rd ed. New York: Free Press.

————, and F. F. Shoemaker. 1971. *Communication of innovations: A crosscultural approach.* Beverly Hills: Sage.

————, and Lawrence Kincaid. 1982. *Communication networks.* New York: Free Press.

Rossiter, Charles, and W. Barnett Pearce. 1975. *Communicating personally.* Indianapolis: Bobbs-Merrill.

Sarti, Ingrid. 1981. Communication and cultural dependency—a misconception. In *Communication and social structure,* edited by E. G. McAnany. New York: Praeger.

Savita. 1970. *Gandhi and the social polity in India.* New Delhi: Institute of Constitutional and Parliamentary Studies.

Schiller, Herbert. 1976. *Communication and cultural domination.* New York: International Arts and Sciences Press.

Schramm, Wilbur. 1978. The nature of comunication between humans. In *The process and effects of mass communication,* 2d ed., edited by W. Schramm and D. F. Roberts, 3–54. Urbana: University of Illinois Press.

————. 1983. The unique perspective of communication: a retrospective view. *Journal of Communication* 33:6–17.

————, and Daniel Lerner. 1976. *Communication and change: The last ten years and the next.* Honolulu: University of Hawaii Press.

Shannon, Claude, and Warren Weaver. 1949. *The mathematical theory of communication.* Urbana: University of Illinois Press.

Shotter, John. 1984. *Social accountability and selfhood.* Oxford: Basil Blackwell.

Silberman, Murray. 1979. Popular participation through communication. *Media Asia* 6:95–101.

Singh, Kusum Jitendra, and Bertram Gross. 1978. Challenges of communication for rural reconstruction. *Media Asia* 6:2–13.

Soedjatmoko. 1976. Development and human needs. Second Ishizaka Memorial Lecture. Compiled by the Indian Institute of Mass Communication, New Delhi.

———. 1978. National policy implications of the basic needs model. Paper presented to the Seminar on Implications of the Basic Needs Model, The Hague.

Sreberny-Mohammadi, Annabelle. 1984. The "world of the news" study. *Journal of Communication* 34:121–34.

Tessier, Elizabeth M., W. Barnett Pearce, William Husson, and Zulkarnaina Mohd. Mess. 1984. Many voices, many worlds: Four readings of the NIIO debate in UNESCO. Paper presented to the International Association for Mass Communication Research, Prague, Czechoslovakia.

Vittal, Nalini. 1981. Communication for rural development. In *Rural development in India—some facets*, edited by S. K. Rau. Hyderabad: National Institute of Rural Development.

Vorys, Karl von. 1975. *Democracy without consensus.* Princeton: Princeton University Press.

Wallerstein, Immanuel. 1979. *The capitalist world economy.* Cambridge: Cambridge University Press.

Watzlawick, Paul, Janet Beavin, and Don Jackson. 1967. *The pragmatics of human communication.* New York: Norton.

Weffort, Francisco C. 1971. *Nota sobre a "teoriada dependecia."* Sao Paulo: Estudos Cebrapl.

UMA NARULA received her Ph.D. in communication from the University of Massachusetts at Amherst in 1983. Since 1967 she has been a research officer with the Indian Institute of Mass Communication, New Delhi; she has published articles on communication, development, and family dynamics. This is her first book.

W. BARNETT PEARCE received his Ph.D. in interpersonal communication from Ohio University in 1969. Chair of the Department of Communication Studies, University of Massachusetts at Amherst, he has published widely on communication. His previous works include *Communicating Personally: A Theory of Interpersonal Communication,* with Charles Rossiter (1975), and *Communication, Action, and Meaning: The Construction of Social Realities,* with Vernon E. Cronen (1980).